Talks With Leaders

Talks With Leaders

Lance Lambert

LANCE LAMBERT MINISTRIES

Richmond, Virginia, USA

ISBN: 978-1-68389-021-8

www.lancelambert.org

Preface

This book, taken from messages given in various places* and at different times, takes us on an instructive, inspirational and challenging tour of true spiritual leadership. Far from the world's idea of position and glory we find a beautiful picture of shepherds who lay down their lives for the flock. They are those anointed by God who have the mind of a bondservant, a hearing ear, a loving shepherd's heart and an approved character.

In light of the strategic times in which we live, may the Lord truly obtain leadership which is according to His mind and ways, "for the perfecting of the saints, unto the work of ministering, unto the building up of the body of Christ" (Ephesians 4:12).

---

* Messages given in Richmond, VA at the Christian Family Conference in the 1980's or at the Halford House in Richmond, Surry, UK.

Contents

Unless otherwise indicated, Scripture quotations
are from the American Standard Version 1901

1.
Leadership in the Church

Regarding the subject of leadership in the church, I do not think I need to underline or emphasize the fact that in the Word of God leadership is given a very important place.

In the kind of Christianity that has developed over the past centuries, one sometimes feels that there is no place for the members of the body; the leader is everything. In fact, in some places the church is considered to be a backdrop to the minster's or pastor's ministry. They are trained as to how to keep their congregation, how to get their support, and how to keep them inspired. It almost seems as if the idea in the New Testament that the church, the body, which is the important thing, has been lost and the means to the end has been made an end in itself.

Now in recent years, praise the Lord, all over the face of the globe there has come a new awareness of the body of Christ. I remember during the years when I first began to preach that when you talked about the church as the body of Christ, people were quite puzzled. They looked at you in a confused and puzzled way as if you had come from the moon with some strange doctrine. The church was some place where you left your Bible, a handbag or an umbrella if you lived in Britain. A church was a place with a steeple or a belfry. If you belonged to another tradition, it was a place that was built as a sacred place of worship in a deliberately ugly manner so that the people of God would not become attached to it. Strangely enough the people of God became attached to the ugly places of worship just as much as to the beautiful ones. But the church was thought of as a place or a building.

Today a revolution has taken place and for this we must thank God. In some quarters it is called "grass roots Christianity." But it is a revolution which I think has brought us back to the beginnings, back to the essential nature of the church being members of Christ and of one another. This thought of the body of the Lord Jesus functioning and being expressed, or of "body ministry" as it is sometimes called, now seems to be a very common topic amongst the people of God. So much so that within institutional and denominational circles there are many such assemblies of God's people who will now consider the whole matter of the functioning of the body.

Not a Free-For-All

Now we are in danger of forgetting the place of leadership because we can go too far in the other direction and become headless so that somehow it is just and only a free-for-all. Everyone therefore does that which is right in their own eyes instead of recognizing the place of leadership. Of course, technically in the New Testament, leadership is expressed by elders in the church.

They are sometimes called elders, which denotes their maturity and wisdom. Another word that is used for them is overseers or bishops—not a bishop, but bishops (plural). This is seen in Philippians 1:1 where the apostle Paul writes to the bishops and deacons in the church which is at Philippi.

Overseers is a very interesting word. The reference to "those who oversee" gives the impression of something developing and growing of itself but that also has to be tended, watched over, and supervised, not in a heavy-handed way but by being overseen. So we have these two wonderful thoughts. On the one side is eldership and on the other side is overseer-ship. Both refer to the same people. Now whether we see the need today that we should have those that we call elders, the fact is that in every company of God's people, especially those who would seek to be a functioning expression of the body of the Lord Jesus, there must be something equivalent to eldership. There must be some kind of leadership.

Of course we are not only talking about eldership because that is the most obvious thing in the New Testament, but there are the deacons as well. In one sense deacons are also leaders. Deacons are men and deaconesses are ladies who care for certain aspects of the life of the church. They oversee those aspects under the leadership of the elders. So this matter actually has no end to it. There is not only, as it were, the leadership of the whole church, the local church, but also those aspects of its life which are also the responsibility of brothers and sisters.

I do hope that we all see just how important this matter is. In these days of growing anarchy and lawlessness, it is even more important that we who belong to the Lord Jesus should understand the necessity and the character of true leadership. We do not want to come into the category of blind leaders of the blind. But when we look at church history, it seems that wherever we look, that which has begun in the spirit has ended in the flesh. That which has begun with true spiritual leadership has ended with blind leaders of the blind. Therefore as we move into the last phase of human history before the coming of the Messiah, we need to see how important it is for the right kind of leadership. I want especially to address those who have responsibility in the things of God, who have some sphere, some department, or some aspect of the life of a company of God's children to care for because I believe that your leadership is absolutely vital.

The Accountability of Leadership

The first thing I would like to underline is the accountability of leadership. God held Eli responsible for his sons. God held Adam responsible for Eve, and God held Saul responsible for the nation. It is no less so in the matter of the house of God. In the old days the high priest and the priesthood were held responsible for anything and everything that happened within the house of God.

Let me put this as clearly as I can: Whatever God commits to you, He holds you accountable for. That is why in the little letter of James it says, "Be not many of you teachers, my brethren, knowing that we shall receive heavier judgment" (James 3:1). In other words, what James was saying by the Spirit of God is, "It is okay if you aspire to be a teacher, but just remember that you have much more for which you are held responsible before God." Better not take on the office than to take it on irresponsibly. If you are a teacher, you are accountable to God as a teacher.

He holds you answerable for that gift, for that function, for that position, and for that responsibility which He has entrusted to you. In II Corinthians Paul says, "For we must all be made manifest before the judgment seat of Christ that each one may receive the things done in the body according to what he hath done whether it be good or bad" (5:10).

In another place the apostle Paul says, "Obey them that have the rule over you and submit to them for they watch in behalf of your souls as they that shall give account, that they may do this with joy and not with grief for this were unprofitable for you" (Hebrews 13:17).

You are accountable. If God has given you a responsibility over the flock of God, if God has given you a responsibility within the household of God, if God has given you a responsibility for the family of God with an overall responsibility of a particular part of His family or a particular aspect of the life of His family in a given place, you are accountable to God for that.

In 1 Corinthians this is how the apostle argues: "Let a man so account of us, as of ministers of Christ, and stewards of the mysteries of God. Here, moreover, it is required in stewards, that a man be found faithful. But with me it is a very small thing that I should be judged of you, or of man's judgment: yea I judge not mine own self. For I know nothing against myself; yet am I not hereby justified: but he that judgeth me is the Lord" (4:1–4).

In Matthew 25:14–28 our Lord told a story of the talents, and this is not to do with salvation as some people think. You will remember that one man was given five talents, one man was given two talents and one man received one talent. The man who had five talents traded them and obtained a further five.

When the master returned he said, "Well done, thou good and faithful servant, enter thou into the joy of thy lord." The man who had two talents also traded them and increased them to four. He also received the same commendation from his lord: "Well done, thou good and faithful servant, enter thou into the joy of thy lord." The one who had only one talent was very afraid. After all he had only one talent and he feared that he might lose it, so instead of trading it he buried it. When the lord returned he said, "Here is your one talent. I knew you were a hard and severe master. I knew you were very conscientious, and so I buried this one talent." Therefore his lord was wrathful and said, "Take away the talent and give it to him who has ten talents." Now this seems terribly unjust: "Oh the poor man has lost his salvation!" No he has not lost his salvation; all he has lost is his place in the government of God. That is all. Those who have learned how to govern, how to really rule in the things of God and how to be responsible are the ones to whom more is given. So to the one who has more shall be given and to the one who has not, even what he has will be taken away.

Accountability is a very important point in this whole matter of leadership. We are accountable for what God has given us. If He has given you a responsibility over the children's work, you are accountable to God for the way you handle that work. If God has given you a responsibility over the finances of a company, you are responsible for the way you handle that before God and to God. If God has given you a responsibility overall, you are accountable to God for that responsibility.

Grace is Commensurate with the Responsibility

Now let us take this matter one step further because it is very important for us to understand. It is not that God has chosen you and you now begin to have a chip on your shoulder and you say, "Why has God made me a leader? I just do not have the equipment. I am inadequate. I am unable to do this. I have the greatest sympathy with the one who went and buried his talent." This is where God catches us out because God never calls a person to a task that He does not give exactly the grace required to fulfill that trust. Furthermore, He does not give someone any gift or responsibility without the measure of faith required to appropriate the grace of the Lord. Both the grace and the faith are commensurate with the gift. If a man is an apostle, he has grace to fulfill his apostolic calling. It is not as though he naturally has something more than others. No, God has given him a calling and therefore has provided the grace necessary for that man to fulfill his apostolic calling and ministry. If a man is a pastor or a teacher, then he has grace to fulfill his ministry as a pastor or a teacher. If a man is an elder, he has grace given to him to fulfill the very difficult responsibility of being an elder amongst the people of God. If you are a help in the body of Christ, then you will have grace to be a help. So there is always grace for the calling. You will not have a great fund of grace for an apostle if you have only been called to be a help. But you will not have grace for being a help if you have been called to be an apostle. This is why God is so severe with us in this matter. In other words, no man ought to be a leader who has not been called by God. There is no substitute for the divine ordination of God. Neither theological seminaries,

Bible colleges, institutional church boards, denominational get-togethers nor anything else can ordain a man for leadership in the work of God if God has not called him. This is where the enemy has done his worst and most terrible work amongst the people of God, insinuating into our midst many men and women who have no business being there. They treat us like the world where it is a matter of ambition, status, office, degrees, or mere physical academic training as though we were Hindus, Buddhists, Muslims or communists! The heart of the matter concerning the church is that it is a divine, a supernatural, and a heavenly organism. It is inexplicable to the natural man and its leadership is produced and created from the right hand of God. It is the Head who appoints men and women and qualifies them in the body of the Lord Jesus.

Ephesians 4:7 says: "But unto each one of us was the grace given according to the measure of the gift of Christ." Please mark these words very carefully. "Unto each one of us was the grace given, according to the measure of the gift of Christ." I hope this is quite clear. That is why when the Lord comes to you, as it were, and holds you accountable for a matter He can be so severe if out of fear you have buried the talent you have been given. You have no business burying the talent. You are accountable because if God has called you, if God has given you a responsibility, He has also given you grace commensurate with that responsibility and therefore you have no excuse.

Grace and Faith

Now the problem is faith. It is one thing to be called, to know that there is grace available, but how to appropriate the grace? We may know as a doctrine that there is grace, but when all the problems and difficulties pile upon us in the matter of leadership, we are forced back into the ways, attitudes and energies of the world. It is also a matter of faith.

Romans 12 says: "For I say, through the grace that was given me, to every man that is among you, not to think of himself more highly than he ought to think; but so to think as to think soberly, according as God hath dealt to each man a measure of *faith*" (v. 3, emphasis author's).

There is not only grace but faith. You are to think soberly, according as God has dealt to you a measure of faith. So here we have both grace and faith.

In this matter of leadership I hope we begin to see one point: None of us ought, in any way, to get involved in leadership in whatever area it is in the church unless God is calling us and obviously qualifying us. (We shall also look at who will be able to distinguish this, whether it be the individual or the church.) Let us be quite clear that one cannot expect to find grace or faith if they are a square peg in a round hole, and there are plenty of them. I know people who have been square pegs in round holes, trying to fit in, for forty or fifty years. Their ministries are as dry as dust. There is no committal of God to them; there is nothing at all. Yet on they go in a kind of endurance test, somehow believing that they ought to be there. It is better to come face to face with the reality in this whole matter. God holds you accountable for the flock over which He has given you responsibility, for the inheritance of the Lord Jesus for which He holds you responsible, and for the outworking of the purpose of God in that local company of believers.

Spiritual Character

The second thing I would like to underline in this matter of leadership in the church is that spiritual character is an all-important factor. Only God can produce leadership. It is not a matter of a title, a matter of a status being given to us, a position into which we are placed, or a training to which we have been subjected. But in the world and I am afraid in very much of Christendom, in Christian things we have adopted the idea of the world that a man may have a totally immoral character but if he is a king, he is a king. The idea being that if we give someone a title, dress them up, and train them, of course they will become qualified.

Leadership is not a question of a title, a status, or a position. It cannot even be produced through training. Listen carefully to me: We can only train what is there. If the leadership quality is there, we can train it. I am not, neither have I ever been, against training. What I am against is the kind of system by which, whether it is a Bible school or theological seminary, we put people through some spiritual sausage machine, turn the thing, and squirt them out the other end. Then out they come sort of fully qualified. They are now servants and ministers of the Lord. They have spent years taking something in like a tape on a tape recorder and now suddenly they are given the degree and out they go. Press the button and it all pours out for years. Sometimes it takes some people seven or eight years to get over their training. They lose all their originality, all their real inward life with God because of this false idea that we can produce servants of the Lord. You cannot produce a servant of the Lord. Only God, the Spirit, can produce a servant of the Lord.

Now, let me point out that training is another matter. There may be a place for Bible training. There may be a place for schooling in the matters of doctrine and of truth and even of practice. Training is a principle we see everywhere in the Word of God. Look how Elijah took Elisha under his wing. Look how the Lord Jesus took the twelve under His wing for three and a half years. Look how the apostle Paul carried a little band around with him. It was his training school on the move, all the time going along with Him. Of course there is this matter of training, but if you and I think we can train into being what is not there in the first place, we are going to end with something superficial, or at the worst, counterfeit. Only God can produce leadership. Once the qualities are there, they are there by the Spirit.

Now they can be marred. I know people who have leadership qualities but because they have never subjected themselves to discipline, never allowed themselves to be corrected, never allowed themselves to be brought into situations where they are broken, and never been able to submit to any kind of authority, their leadership amounts in value to nil. We can dissipate what God intends for you and for me. But this matter of spiritual character is all important and that is why we have this tremendous emphasis within the Word of God in the New Testament on the matter of example.

Examples to the Flock

On the other side of the Atlantic we are quite used to shepherds and sheep, and in Israel it is part of daily life. Every now and again a shepherd trails a whole lot of sheep almost right through our front door. It is a very funny thing to be in a capital city and to see sheep going all the way across town with shepherds just like they have done for three thousand years. However, there is a difference between European and Israeli shepherds. The European shepherds follow the sheep and usually have dogs running around doing the work ahead, whereas Israeli shepherds normally speaking do not like dogs and the Bedouin shepherds most certainly do not like them. Therefore you will see some little lad who is a shepherd boy out in front with two hundred sheep and goats all following him—wherever the shepherd goes, the sheep and the goats go. It is a most extraordinary sight. They lead the sheep.

In the armies of the Western world, American, European, and British officers stay in the back. This is not to be taken as any hit at the establishment, but normally the officers sit at the back and the men die in the front. One of the bitter things in every battle is that the men die in their thousands in the front while all the officers remain safely in the background. Of course there is a military strategy involved because of the need to keep the officer class. They must be kept (although some of the soldiers might wonder whether they are worth keeping sometimes!) Nevertheless, the idea behind it is that of preserving the brains because if you destroy them you may lose the battle.

Now in the Bible and in modern Israel the tradition that officers must lead their men is still followed. That is why in every one of the Israeli battles and wars there are an enormous number of casualties, relatively speaking, among the officers. They have to lead their men into battle. They never stay in the background; they always go in the front with the men following.

It is very important for us to understand what God means by leadership because He does not want leaders who stay in the background directing everything from some safe vantage point, but He wants men who are examples, who are pioneers. If leaders speak of faith, they must be pioneers of faith. If they speak of devotion, they must be pioneers of devotion. If they speak of sacrifice, they must be pioneers in sacrifice. If they speak of humility, they themselves must be pioneers or examples of humility. That is why we have so much in the Word of God about examples. Let me give a few scriptures having to do with elders:

"The elders among you I exhort, who am a fellow-elder, and a witness of the sufferings of Christ, who am also a partaker of the glory that shall be revealed: Tend the flock of God which is among you, exercising the oversight, not of constraint, but willingly, according to the will of God; nor yet for filthy lucre, but of a ready mind; neither as lording it over the charge allotted to you, but making yourselves ensamples to the flock. And when the chief Shepherd shall be manifested, ye shall receive the crown of glory that fadeth not away" (1 Peter 5:1–4).

Be examples to the flock. Not lording it over them, not becoming petty little dictators in your own little empire, but ensamples to the flock. In 1 Timothy chapter 3 we realize it is all to do with elders and deacons. But here is the interesting thing: it is not to do with the techniques, the methods, or the pattern; it is all to do with character. If we read very carefully through it, we find that the apostle Paul is saying, "Now make sure that elders have this kind of character and it is the same regarding the deacons." In Titus we have exactly the same thing: "If any man is blameless, the husband of one wife, having children that believe, who are not accused of riot or unruly. For the bishop must be blameless, as God's steward; not self-willed, not soon angry, no brawler, no striker, not greedy of filthy lucre; but given to hospitality, as lover of good, sober-minded, just, holy, self-controlled; holding to the faithful word which is according to the teaching, that he may be able to exhort in the sound doctrine, and to convict the gainsayers" (1:6–9).

In Acts 20, when the apostle Paul is speaking to the elders of the church before he sets sail from them in Miletus and Ephesus, he says: " In all things I gave you an example, that so laboring ye ought to help the weak, and to remember the words of the Lord Jesus, that he himself said, It is more blessed to give than to receive" (v.35).

In 1 Timothy we read: "Let no man despise thy youth; but be thou an ensample to them that believe, in word, in manner of life, in love, in faith, in purity" (4:12).

Take Heed to Yourselves

In connection with this may I make another remark which I think is sometimes overlooked. So important is this matter of spiritual character in those who are leaders that we have a very interesting little word attached to this matter of responsibility in the church.

Indeed people take it as a message for all and sundry, but it is the little word take heed to yourself. Now I find that very interesting. Let us look again at Acts 20:28 and pay attention to the words: *"Take heed unto yourselves,* and to all the flock, in which the Holy Spirit hath made you bishops, to feed the church of the Lord which he purchased with his own blood"* (author's emphasis).

He did not just simply say as we would expect, "Take heed to the flock of which the Lord has made you overseers!" He said, "Take heed to yourselves and to the flock." Give your own life as much attention. Do not think that you yourself may not fall. Rather think that because of the position into which God has led you the enemy would work even more to bring you down. You can talk to others of devotion and your own devotion can grow cold. You can talk to others about faith and the necessity of faith and you yourself no longer exercise faith. You yourself may talk to others about purity and your mind is filled with evil thoughts. You can talk to others about single heartedness, and you are double minded and unstable. You did not begin that way, but that is how you have become. There is a saying that power corrupts and total power corrupts totally.

It is very true that when we are young in the things of God and in the service of God we can be so lean. There is no excess flesh; we are spiritually athletic, spiritually flexible, and spiritually alert. But then when we take up responsibility and God is with us and we begin to see things developing, we can become lax. Somehow the tragedy is that in the end we are tripped up.

Take another scripture in this matter: 1 Timothy 4:16 says: "Take heed to thyself, and to thy teaching." This is a very interesting word about teaching. I just mention this again in passing:

How easy it is when we are young in the Lord and have the fear of God to be very careful about what we teach, and how dangerous it is when once we have an accepted and popular ministry to begin to allow error to creep into our teaching. Some of us could say so much about movements that I think began in the Spirit which have gone right off the rails on this very matter. Take heed to thyself and to thy teaching. Never think that because God has been with you, is with you, and is committed to you that the enemy could not seduce you or that some kind of doctrine of demons could not be insinuated into your ministry—take heed to yourself and to your teaching.

Of course, there are other well-known scriptures that are not specifically to do with leadership but in general they relate to this matter. I refer to 1 Corinthians 10:12: "Wherefore let him that thinketh he standeth take heed lest he fall." Or Galatians 6:1: "Brethren, even if a man be overtaken in any trespass, ye who are spiritual, restore such a one in a spirit of gentleness; looking to thyself lest thou also be tempted." Therefore spiritual character in this matter of leadership is all—important.

The Work of the Holy Spirit

The third thing I want to underline is the emergence of leadership in the church. It is a very interesting thing and I well remember the shock with which it first came to me, when I discovered that the apostle Paul never appointed elders on his first missionary journey. Now if we think about this for a few moments, he could have easily done it. After all he had begotten those churches everywhere and they were thriving in a great spiritual condition.

Why could he not take Silas, Timothy, Barnabas or somebody else and go aside for a few days of prayer and fasting? Then the Lord would say, "Now then, So-and-so, So-and-so, and So-and-so are the leaders." Then they could have come forward and said, "By revelation, God has shown us that you, you and you are leaders!" and they could have been right.

Paul would have done untold damage to the spiritual growth of those brothers if they had been recognized too early. It was on his return journey (which of course is nothing like today where we can take a plane somewhere, have a great time of fellowship and ministry and then return), that he appointed elders. In the olden days the way the apostle traveled would have taken anywhere between nine to eighteen months in a journey right the way round. It was on the way back that he appointed elders when time had been given for the organic development of the church. The scripture for that is Acts 14:23: "And when they had appointed for them elders in every church, and had prayed with fasting, they commended them to the Lord, on whom they had believed."

But I want to add to it another very interesting verse found in Titus 1:5: "For this cause left I thee in Crete, that thou shouldest set in order the things that were wanting, and appoint elders in every city, as I gave thee charge."

Now I find this very interesting. Why did the apostle Paul not say to Titus, "Now Titus, I am going to have to leave and I think it would be a very good idea if we now had a time of waiting upon the Lord and fasting and we will get clearly from the Lord those that ought to be the right men"? I have no doubt they must have talked and prayed about it and probably even discussed names at some point, but instead he left Titus behind in order to allow for the organic development of leadership. Do not over-quickly recognize leadership. That is why in another place the apostle Paul says, "Lay hands hastily on no man, neither be partaker of other men's sins" (1 Timothy 5:22a). Now that does not mean, as some I think have wondered, that you must never sort of box the ears of somebody or roughly take hold of them. It means that you do not recognize somebody's office, ministry or position in the household of God too quickly. Do not do it hastily; rather wait.

Leadership always emerges through the work of the Holy Spirit. He is the one who is the custodian of the things of God and He in particular is in charge of the house of God.

Now how do we see these things? I am quite sure that if it is just a question of a small matter within the church, there are things which we can take up and can also drop. People get into a great sweat over this whole thing. They say, "Oh, but you have just said we are accountable to God! I dare not 'look after' giving everyone a cup of coffee at the end of a time of fellowship! Not unless the Lord calls me." I would have thought it was sufficient if one or two brethren approached someone and said, "Could you do this?" And they said, "Yes, I will."

It is most interesting that a great argument arose in the early church, which of course was all Jewish. In the very beginning they were divided into two types of Jews that I have often thought were rather like British and Americans. There were the "go-ahead" Greek-speaking Jews who were always in front of every great drive forward anywhere in the whole Roman Empire and the very conservative orthodox Hebrew-speaking Jews who were always holding everything back. They tended to be the deeper ones but they were rather stuffy. Now an argument grew up within the early church about the distribution of money to the widows. The Greek-speaking widows said, "We are not getting the food we should be getting! They are feeding all those Hebrew-speaking widows first and when it comes to us there is no more!" (see Acts 6:1). So the church waited on God. The apostles said, "Let us wait on the Lord," and they together set aside seven men. Now the interesting thing was that every one of those men belonged to the Greek-speaking Jews (everyone has a Greek name, Acts 6:5–6). I thought it was a very beautiful thing on the part of the Hebrew-speaking Jewish believers that they said, "All right, we will appoint the ones of the opposition."

But the most interesting thing is that it seems these people did not remain in their offices for too long. Soon one of them called Philip is a flaming evangelist going all round holding great meetings, and hundreds are being saved! We find him going out into the desert by the Spirit of God, meeting the Ethiopian eunuch and bringing him to the Lord (see Acts 8). Then there is Stephen, one of the greatest teachers the church has known. Some people believe that Stephen's words actually underlie the letter of the Hebrews. If Stephen had lived, he would have been the peer of the apostle Paul in teaching ability and understanding. How interesting this all is. Evidently the distribution of the funds and food was not a job for life, but a kind of training ground, a testing ground almost, and once they proved faithful, the Holy Spirit moved them into something far more valuable.

Recognizing the Emergence of Leadership

How do we recognize the emergence of leadership? In principle it seems that there are two things involved. One is that the church itself recognizes something. I do not believe that there are ever leaders within the church that the church does not (if it is a company of spiritual people) intuitively recognize. The church is amazing in its own way. They can be very young, they can be failing, they can be many things that are not right, and yet somehow within the church, if it really is the church, there is a collective intuition about people and about things. I think that is quite important.

The other thing is that it seems there has to be recognition from brethren who have responsibility greater than local. In other words, as I see it in the Word, especially in leadership, there are brethren that are able to confirm what the church really feels. Therefore it is like a marriage. Something is terribly wrong in a marriage when a husband has to continually say to his wife that she must be subject to him. When people continually have to read the riot act[1] to one another, something is wrong. When wives have to moan and groan about husbands who do not love them, something is wrong. Where you have to throw the book at them and sort of say, "You see what it says?! Husbands! Love your wives!" there is something terribly wrong. In a happy relationship I think many a word that a wife whispers is taken as Papal infallibility. She does not have to bawl at the top of her voice, "This and this should be done!" she only has to whisper something and somehow the husband feels it is his own idea. Is it

---

1 An expression reffering to the Act of Parliament

not so? When there is a really good relationship, it is a relationship of love and order. It is a relationship in which you do not have to often define the various sides. It is only when it breaks down that we have to clearly say, "Look, something has gone wrong. You should be this and you should be that." It seems to me that in the church it is very much like that. There is an intuition within a company of God's people as to those who have the right qualities and calling. They feel it inside the company and the recognition is confirmed in the appointment by those outside.

Leadership Qualities

How can we recognize leadership qualities? I will list seven questions and I must say that I find it very difficult to find myself in the qualifications; nevertheless I shall present them in order to help us understand how we can recognize leadership qualities.

Is There an Anointing?

First of all, is there an anointing of God on him or her? I put that first. Now I am not asking whether they have had some experience that knocked them out for forty-eight hours so that they lay on the floor and could say nothing. I am not asking whether they have been caught up to the third heaven and heard things that are not lawful to utter. I am asking this: Does God come down on what they say and do? Does He come through what they say and do? It is the difference between chalk and cheese—between those leaders who are under the anointing and those of whom we are conscious that what they say and do is merely human. What they say is human and what they do is human, but somebody else can say the same words in the Spirit, and immediately we are in the presence of the Lord. This is not a natural charisma. It was Spurgeon who once said, "If a man is going to preach, God does not take a man with half a lung." In other words, when God is going to use a person to really teach, as in the early church for example, He takes a brain like the apostle Paul and then breaks him. He then puts his brain back together under the anointing of the Holy Spirit and then we have something. The brain itself can do nothing in the things of God. But when God takes the brain and puts it through the death, burial and resurrection of Jesus and into the anointing of God by the Spirit, then He has a brain. So it is with everything.

Is there an anointing of God in him or her? Is he filled with the Spirit? Although he is not speaking of leadership in the local church, the apostle Paul says in one or two places "Am I lacking in signs or wonders that I did amongst you that are the evidence of my apostleship?" (I Corinthians 9:2; II Corinthians 12:12). When a man is called, there is evidence that he is called, no matter how small it is. There are some people who are looking after different aspects of the work of this conference, and the way they do it brings one face to face with the Lord. Other people can do the same job and all you see is them; but oh the difference when somebody does it under the anointing! Then it is God who comes down upon it and through it. So I repeat, is he or she filled with the Spirit?

Is it not interesting that there was nobody given the task of distributing food amongst quarreling widows who was not filled with the Spirit?! It seems to me that if the qualification for serving the table was they had to be filled with the Spirit to even fulfill so small a function as distributing food, where are we?

Is there a Basic Faithfulness?

Here is my second question: Is there a basic faithfulness? I Corinthians 4:2 says: "Moreover, it is required in stewards that a man be found faithful." Does he or she give the Lord absolute priority? Is there no expediency and no compromise? Does he or she finish what he or she begins? Is there a basic faithfulness in him or her?

Is there an Essential Meekness?

Thirdly, is there an essential meekness? II Timothy 2:25 says, "In meekness correcting them that oppose." Now what is meekness? Meekness is to be teachable. Is he or she teachable? Why is it that when people become leaders they become unteachable? How is it that some small member of the family cannot teach them something? It is because of a basic insecurity and fear. There is a feeling of inadequacy so that they cannot receive from anybody lest they lose face in front of them. But the meek person can learn from anybody.

Does he or she have a hearing ear? Have they themselves submitted to authority? Is there an essential meekness in him or her?

Is there a Serving Attitude?

Fourthly, is there a serving attitude toward everyone? In Mark 10:42–45 the Lord said, "Do not lord it over them as the Gentiles love to lord it over one another. But be servants, bond slaves, one to another." He then goes on and says: "For the Son of man also came not to be ministered to but to minister [to serve], and to give his life a ransom for many."

Is there a serving attitude toward everyone? Is he or she a servant or a boss? A minister or a dictator? Is there a life laid down or an ambition promoted?

Is the Love of God the Constraining Factor?

Fifthly, is the love of God the constraining factor? II Corinthians 5:14 says: "The love of Christ constrains us." What motivates him or her? Is it ambition? Power? Success? Self-fulfillment or self-satisfaction? Now let me get this quite clear: There is nothing wrong with ambition. I do not know if there has ever been a great leader in the history of the church that at some point probably did not have some ambition to be somebody or something. Again, it is a question of whether God has been able to break that of the sting within.

There is an idea among some believers that we all must be ninnies. They want to take out the back bone and make us all weak, pale and anemic. Such a one might say: "No, no I do not want to do anything. I do not want to be here; I do not want anything at all." But that is not right. You cannot be good soldiers of Jesus Christ enduring hardship and be like some of the ninnies that pass for Christians. They have the idea that meekness is weakness. There is a kind of self-affliction and severity to the flesh. There is approval if one looks sort of anemic, poor and broken. It is nonsense! These people have wills like iron. They sit (forgive me) in the back row and look as though saying: "We don't want anything." But boy, do they make their feelings and their will known in every single thing that happens in the church. They are the first to collide with anybody. I would rather have one of those dreadful fleshly types of people who is full of ambition and says, "I want to boss the lot!" and then God gets hold of him and breaks him. If we had known Saul of Tarsus before he was saved, I imagine that man had ambition. He was like a flaming fire, like a meteor, until God paralyzed him and he then became the great apostle.

I am only saying this to correct any false idea that means we do not have any ambition. We just sit there doing nothing, we become passive little ninnies who never open our mouths, never wanting to know anything—it is nonsense! The Book says, "He who desires the office of a bishop, desires a good thing" (1 Timothy 3:1); but then it says, "Make love your aim" (1 Corinthians 14:1). Such ambition has to be dealt with. Nevertheless this question remains: Is the love of God the constraining factor? A man cannot help having ambition if he is ambitious by nature. But if the love of God has entered into him, then there is all the glorious possibility that God will take him to a place where he will meet his waterloo, his end, and come out the other side in reality as a new man in Christ.

Perfect love casts out fear and insecurity. I think there is an awful lot of insecurity amongst leaders. That is why they snap and snarl. That is why they get all funny when challenged on anything and why some of them cannot take any criticism or suggestion. It is a basic feeling of inadequacy and insecurity.

When God has called us, we can take it all to God as Moses did; we can fall on our faces before the Lord and say, "Now Lord, what shall we do?"

Is There a Purity of Heart?

Sixthly, is there a purity of heart? Matthew 5:8 says: "Blessed are the pure in heart: for they shall see God." Are there unsettled issues in that life? I am referring to serious and basic issues. Now all of us will have issues throughout life, but are there basic issues unsettled in that life? Is there double mindedness? Are they seeking to serve God and mammon?

May I say this as an encouragement? Most people think of Jacob as the most twisted character in the whole Book. He is the one whom we would think of as the most opposite to being pure in heart, yet he saw God. I contend that deeper than all the twistedness of his nature, Jacob actually was pure in heart. Deep down he wanted God and the things of God with all his heart. The trouble was the way he tried to get them. When finally he saw the Lord face to face and lived, he was a different man and became a prince with God and with men. Just because we have problems does not mean that deep down within our being we do not have a heart for God. Thus it is that which finally brings a person through.

Is There a Life Laid Down?

Lastly, is his or hers a life laid down? When a person has laid down their life, they have laid down their life. They do not take it up again. A person who took up their cross was a person whose life was already over. They had no compromises and no issues to settle; their life was over. There were just a short few steps from the sentence to the place of execution. That is what Jesus meant when He said, "If any man follow me, let him deny himself, or give up all right to himself, take up his cross and follow me." Therefore we have to ask: Is his or hers a life laid down?

These questions help us to distinguish whether or not the qualities of leadership are in a person. The standard is very high, but only God knows the kind of standard we need in these days.

2.
Questions & Answers

We have a number of questions that have been asked on this matter of leadership in the church. Quite a few of these questions overlap one another so I hope that in answering one or two of them it will answer some of the others as well.

Q:

We are a relatively new and young gathering of believers, thirty to forty of us and only two couples who are over forty years old, everyone else is about thirty or younger. At the present we have had only three brothers minister to us from outside in the eighteen months we have been together. Two of the younger brothers come from a gathering in a nearby city that teaches that you cannot have a church without elders and that they are appointed or ordained by the laying on of hands by an apostle. These brothers are very anxious to have elders appointed by a brother who ministered to us whom they regard as an apostle and I believe that they would like for us to regard him as our apostle. Several of us are very uncomfortable with this. Presently we have a

meeting of brethren who have taken responsibility for the gathering.
This has been articulated to the brethren and they seem to be okay
with this arrangement so far. With this information, and assuming
that my background is similar to the teachings of the conference
[the Christian Family Conference], would you please comment on
this situation that would help me and many of us who are here and
answer any or all of the following questions?"

A:

Now the questions are good because they are asked by many
others as well. First of all, how important is the form? The great
question is whether in the recovery of the church we expect or
look for a complete and absolute recovery of the church to the "nth"
degree, that is, that it should return to the exact conditions that we
had in the first century during the period of the New Testament.
I personally do not believe that there will be a recovery of the
church in that way; however there are those who do believe that
and if they are right, I should be very happy.

It was Mark Twain who once said "we learn from history that
we never learn from history." But if I take the course of revealed
history according to God's Word, then I find that whereas in every
age things began with everybody being involved, they end always
with only a remnant who are completing or fulfilling the mind of
God for that time. There are those who believe that there will be
a total apostasy in the church. They say there will come a falling
away in the church, in the house of God, that the love of the many
will wax cold, and that when the Lord comes to the earth He will
not find faith. In other words there will be a complete break up
and break down of everything of God. I personally do not agree

with this because just where we would least expect to find it in the book of Revelation after there have been all the visions of Babylon, the dragon, the beast, the serpent and so on, we find this: "Hallelujah: for the Lord our God, the Almighty, reigns. Let us rejoice and be exceeding glad... for the marriage of the Lamb is come, and his wife hath made herself ready" (Revelation 19:6b–7).

I often think that the expression the bride hath made herself ready is marvelous because it is not good Reform Doctrine. If we were to follow Reform Doctrine we would have to say, and the bride has been made ready. But it says, "and the bride has made herself ready." I think that the Holy Spirit has deliberately put that there for our encouragement, showing that right at the time of the end there will be a marvelous energy of the Spirit of God released into the believers so that the bride is completed and the purpose of God is fulfilled. So there is another side to the coin.

The question is, what are we looking for? It seems to me that we must look for a moving of the Spirit of God upon believers who really see what the Lord's heart's desire is and who commit themselves one hundred percent to the Lord and to His purpose for our day and generation. This is not elitism. When we come together, as we say, on "church ground" (this term has been misused in some parts and I hardly like to use it), when we come together really on the basis of Christ, we are returning to the original foundation upon which God built the church. That does not mean we are marvelous people. There may be far better people among the Southern Baptists, the Methodists, the Presbyterians, or in some charismatic group. But it so happens that God has shown us something and wanting to be faithful and obedient, we will come together on that ground. We may be the poorest of the lot but at least we will come together on that ground.

Now we have a problem and the problem is whether there is this cast-iron legalistic concept of the church or whether it is understood to be organic. If you hold this cast-iron Universalist idea, which I believe is at the root of the problem with the Exclusive Brethren and the problem with the Local Church Movement, then you have a cast-iron system very much like the papacy. You have built up a system in which you are the church in such and such a place. Therefore if you are the church in a given place, you can have the elders.

On the other hand, surely the Lord who understands that at the end of the age it will not be the same as it was in the beginning with every believer involved, surely there must be those who represent elders. In other words, surely it is not beyond the Holy Spirit to adapt himself to the situation in which we are found. I personally would be a little afraid of making a big thing about elders and deacons, although I personally am not afraid of calling people "elder brothers" and "deacons." If a person is actually fulfilling the function, he is fulfilling the function of a deacon or an elder. So what does it matter? Why do people get into such a mess over this? It is as if the title is all important. When I have a doctor dealing with me I do not care whether he calls himself "Doctor So-and-so," as long as I know he has gone through medical school, is qualified and has had some experience. If a man is an elder we may or may not call him an elder but he is an elder. If we all get tied up on the question of titles, status and position, we do great injustice to this whole matter. The real issue is that we must have the function. So the question is: How important is the form of eldership as compared to the function? I would say the all-important matter is the function. It always has been. It is not as though in the New Testament the important thing was the form. The important thing was the function. Therefore I think this is a very important point. Whatever we call those who have responsibility for leadership in the flock, the fact remains that the Holy Spirit will adapt Himself to the conditions which are found today in the last part of the twentieth century.

Q:

What is the best way for a gathering like ours to go under the conditions I described?

A:

I believe that what was said about having a meeting of brethren who have taken responsibility for the gathering is a very good idea. I do not quite understand this concept that you cannot have a church without elders. Who said it? It goes back to this cast-iron concept of the church which becomes a papal system where you must have a kind of top-heavy thing. You cannot have a church unless you have elders and deacons and so on. It seems to me that a church is where two or three believers, saved by the grace of God and who have been positioned in the Lord Jesus by God, come together. That is a church.

We will begin with this concept that you may not have any elders or deacons. In the New Testament they did not have them in the very beginning. Jerusalem had apostles at the very start, and before long we find that they had elders and James was the presiding elder as such. When you go to another place where two or three people got saved, what does the apostle do when he leaves? Does he say, "Now you are not a church"? Then what are they? Who are they? So they are nothing? Someone says, "No, you must wait until you are thirty or forty strong, then you will be a church. You must have a certain quorum before you can be a church." Others would say, "No, before you can be a church, you must have elders." Someone else would say, "No, no, no, you must have elders and deacons." And someone else says, "No, no, the thing that matters is that you must have the Lord's Table." Of course, all these things develop in time. One would expect if there was a church in Antioch or a church in Ephesus, Sardis, or somewhere else, that as it moved on with God these things would emerge. Whether they break bread every day or whether they have the Lord's Table once a month or once a week, whether they have the Lord's Table on Saturday evening, Sunday morning, Sunday evening or Thursday evening, does not really matter. The church is the body of Christ. If it so happens that in one village or town there are only three believers to begin with, it may only be the church in embryonic form, but it is still the church of God there in the New Testament sense. When we all get tied up on this matter of elders and deacons, it is amazing. I do not know any matter that ties up a new young company of believers more than this matter of elders, deacons, apostles and all the rest of it. The real business is to grow in the Lord.

In the meantime it does seem that you must have some brethren take responsibility. It might be good at the beginning to open it to more brethren rather than less because if you have just one or two, automatically it may be very difficult for them to give way if other leadership were to develop amongst them. This is a big problem.

Ambition is a problem. It is especially so in the man more than the woman. In spite of all this teaching about total equality I do not think the ladies have quite the same ambitious instincts that men have. It is a real problem when you get a collection of men together who are normal and virile. They are ambitious and they all want to be something. Therefore, when you raise the matter of eldership, it is like waving a red rag in front of bulls and they all sort of see red and start up.

I personally think it is best to make the point that if men are going to lead the church, it is not a pyramid with the apostles and elders at the top sitting on the whole church in all their glory demanding obedience. Rather we have to invert the pyramid so that the whole weight of the church comes onto these men. If we can get that concept over to believers, suddenly we see it in terms of service and sacrifice. Then the question of apostolic ministry or the question of eldership or leadership becomes in many ways a sacrificial laying down of the life, a bearing of the burden of the whole.

Q:

Speak about the qualification of elders, especially in view of the youthfulness of our gathering.

A:

Do you honestly think that the Holy Spirit has been taken by surprise? So He suddenly says, "Oh my goodness! They are all young! I did not realize that when I led them to the Lord Jesus! Then when I led them together, I was not thinking. Now we have a whole collection of young people, all less than thirty years of age and only two couples that are over forty! Oh dear, dear, I have made a mess of this!"

You may laugh because once it is put to you it is so silly. It is not as though the Holy Spirit says, "Oh dear, what are we going to do about this?" The Holy Spirit knows exactly the constituency of any given company of God's people. If it so happens that you are all young people, the leadership is going to be young. And if we take the only older ones amongst us we may make a big mistake. Just because a person is old with white or grey hair does not mean they have wisdom. Some of them are as dumb as they come. Now I do not want to say that unkindly because it is very wrong to despise white hair. However, the fact remains that in spiritual things we have learned, to our great sorrow, that whereas it ought to be that if a person is old that they have wisdom and know the Lord, it does not follow.

I must say that in the work in Richmond, England, we got all our trouble from the "over-fifties." Mercifully we had only a few of them. But my word! They were the cross to all of us! They disrupted our meetings, they contradicted what we had found together before God, they always knew best, they were always telling us where we were going wrong, and frankly, they were wrong. If we had followed their advice, we would have been in a terrible mess. In fact at the very beginning of the work in Richmond we made the terrible mistake of making one of these men who was a very successful businessman as well as older than all of us by a generation, an elder. Oh boy! De-elderizing him was one of the biggest jobs we ever had. That was in the very early days of the work in Richmond, and we learned one of our big mistakes through this matter.

You do not even appoint people through prayer and fasting. That is what we did and then we selected three people because we thought the prayer and fasting had sanctified any decision we might make. It is nonsense of course, because the emergence of leadership is organic and the selection of leadership is related to the organic development of that company and of those ones. Therefore in answer to the question regarding qualifications of an elder, I do not think they have changed. They may be found in Timothy or Titus. Basically they are people with spiritual character and spiritual vision who have laid down their lives for the church of God and have proven it.

Now someone will say to me, "But doesn't it say that you must be married?" I do not think so. If I understand correctly, it says they must be the husband of one wife (1 Timothy 3:2). In fact, it was still common, as it has been until this century, for Oriental Jews to have more than one wife; but they were not allowed to take responsibility if they had more than one wife. That was following the Old Testament pattern. It does not mean that someone who is single cannot be an elder, although the general pattern would be that elders were to be married men who have families and have experience of family life, as well as having experience of life, and above all having experience of the Lord.

The question of "elders" plural, does not just mean physical years, it means spiritual years. In other words, it means spiritual experience. Now does that mean because a person has been converted twenty years and here is a brother who has been converted seven years we should choose the brother who is twenty years old in the Lord? No, not at all. I know people who have been converted thirty-five years and they are spiritual babes.

They know no more than when they began. They have been carried all their days. I also know some who are only four or five years old in the Lord and who will outstrip them because they have grown up in wisdom, stature and in a knowledge of the Lord. However, we have to be careful. The Bible says we should never pick someone who is a novice, that is, someone who is just newly saved and very young in the Lord (1 Timothy 3:2).

Q:

Do you believe there is any age restriction on leadership? By age I mean both physical and spiritual years? I ask this in light of all of the apostles having sat for over three years before serving. All of those who waited on the Hebrew widows sat for eight to ten years and Paul himself sat ten years, four of which were under Barnabas.

A:

Now this raises another question about the matter of leadership, and it is a very good one. I think that this is a point well made. The apostles had been three and a half years under the leadership of the Lord Jesus; however, I am afraid at the end of the three years, most of it was skin deep. It was the coming of the Holy Spirit upon them and into them that turned it all inside and brought them to an inward knowledge. Still those three and half years were invaluable. When they chose the twelfth apostle in place of Judas Iscariot, the one point they made was that 'he must have been with us all and with the Lord for three and a half years' (Acts 1:31–32). I think this matter of training is quite important, and the point about Paul being with Barnabas is well taken. I do not think that any person can be an elder or a leader who has not himself been led. If it is quite clear that he has not been led, however brilliant and clever the brother is, I think it is dangerous to give responsibility to such a one.

We have to prove that we can take orders and do them, that we can submit to discipline, and that we ourselves can be under authority if authority is going to be exercised by us. I think that is quite an important point. So in this matter of the qualifications for elders I would certainly include this matter of a period of time in which a person has proven himself in the eyes of the church and in the eyes of other brethren, perhaps with wider responsibilities than the local church, that he really is a man led of God.

Q:

What about outside ministry and help to confirm the brothers as they are recognized as elders by the brothers. We lack that now, what do we do?

You shared with us how important it is that the local leadership have the confirmation of a brother other than local of their calling into responsibility. Does this imply that every local gathering should find a kind of covering and leadership outside of their locality, maybe apostolic ministry? How and why, if so? In other words, what is an apostle and how does a locality recognize him?

A:

Here we come into a very, very difficult sphere. Let me say this straightaway. There are people who say there is no such thing as apostolic ministry today. I have the most serious question about such a statement. It is perfectly true that the twelve apostles are in a category of their own, but even so we have others referred to as apostles such as Apollos, Titus and Timothy who did not come into that category (I Corinthians 4–6; II Corinthians 8:23; Romans 16:21). Whatever we might say about the passing away of apostleship with the New Testament canon of Scripture and its completion, the fact remains that in every single move of the Holy Spirit right down through the history of the church there has always been not only the local but those with wider responsibilities. Are we aware of a single move in the recovery of the church where there were not brethren moving amongst the churches? It does not matter whether it was the Reformers, the Quakers, the Wesleyans or the Brethren. The Brethren in particular were a little sticky on some of these things, but in the heyday when the whole thing was a recovery of church life there were Brethren who moved full-time between the companies continually. Later on in Brethren circles it became a kind of "thing." Sadly it has changed because they have lost some of their earliest understanding, but when I remember the Brethren in the 1950's, they would not have any full-time ministry. They said everyone had to have a job. Now the fact of the matter is if we look at church history we find apostolic ministry all the way through from beginning to end. Again we may not call them apostles, but the function is there, and it seems to me that you cannot have anything healthy without that function.

Once again we come into great problems. First of all, I think it is very dangerous if one man has a kind of apostolic position in which he simply holds churches in his hands. Even when the apostle Paul had founded churches, Apollos came through and complemented his ministry and Peter came through as well and complemented Paul's ministry. There was a marvelous interweaving of different apostolic ministries. You will remember that Paul said you may have "ten thousand tutors" but you have only one father, meaning that he begat that church (I Corinthians 4:15). Therefore, if someone has spiritually begotten churches, he has a relationship to those churches which no one else has. However, the danger is of that relationship becoming papal. Then it becomes a strait jacket, an inhibiting factor upon the growth of those companies. If, on the other hand, other brethren can come in and give what they have of the Lord with the same type of authority, then the whole thing can be balanced in a most healthy manner.

The New Testament makes it quite clear that the apostles, or at least the work, appointed elders in the churches. What do we do today? It seems to me that we must find our way by following the Lord. The following statement relayed by Miss Fishbacher has always helped me. She told me years ago that brother Nee once said, "If the Ark of the Covenant and the tent of the meeting ever get parted, do not follow the tent of the meeting; follow the Ark of the Covenant." That would have saved us many problems throughout the years if we had done so. These two things should never be divorced: the tent of meeting and the Ark of the Covenant. But if there ever comes a time when the Ark of the Covenant, which represents the presence of God, the Testimony of Jesus, should be taken away, and the tent of meeting divorced from it, do not follow the tent of meeting, follow the ark. That seems applicable in these days of breakdown and so much error. In days when the Lord is seeking to recover, if only in a remnant of His people, some of these marvelous church principles, then let us follow the ark not the tent of meeting. If we will just follow the Lord He will surely find a way through. He knows what is happening and I think this would be much better than some company rooting all around the southeast of the United States for an apostle and possibly ending up with a man who might destroy the work. I think it would be much better for them to follow the Lord and spend hours in prayer together on their knees and let the Holy Spirit lead them. The Holy Spirit is well able to adapt in times of breakdown or even contradiction and so lead His children into what He wants.

However, there are brethren with a wider responsibility in the church. I would always advise any company to never put itself into the hands of a man whose life is not totally laid down for the Lord and for His people. There is so much personal empire building, bringing things into power complexes, all dressed up in New Testament terms and phraseology. I would be very careful. I would want to see in a brother some fruit of a life laid down, of a sacrificial service and of a real bearing of the burdens of the church before putting yourselves into his hands.

Q:

Regarding the role or function of an apostle in this matter—do apostles even exist in the spiritual sense in the United States today?

A:

I would hope and trust that there is such a thing as an apostolic function in the United States and in Canada today. I do hope that there are brethren who really are functioning in that way before

God. Whether or not we call them apostles matters not. The fact is that we need the function if the house of God is to function.

Q:

What about the use of expressions such as "fellowship" instead of "gathering" or "assembly"? Should we call ourselves a church? We feel we are a part of the church, not "it."

A:

I think the last point is what should be underlined. We are part of the church. Those who meet together in Richmond on the foundation of the Lord Jesus and seeking to really experience church life may feel very poor. They may feel they have many mistakes, but at least they are seeking to meet together in Christ and on no other ground to really experience something of church life.

If we say we are the church I think we have come into a very serious complex. So what do we call ourselves? Here we have a problem. I do not know that gathering is actually more Scriptural than fellowship and I must point out that the New Testament does not use the word fellowship as the fellowship. Fellowship is a description, not a title. So nowhere in the New Testament do we find it used as the fellowship, for example the fellowship at Antioch, or the fellowship at Ephesus. It does not say that, but neither does it say the gathering.

Mr. Sparks loved the word gathering and we used it very much because of our Honor Oak background. We would say "the gathering of the Lord's people here" or "the gathering of the Lord's people there." It is a rather lovely word portraying believers gathering together in Christ. But it is no more New Testament than fellowship if we want to be technical and legal because the word is not used quite like that.

Then there is the word assembly which is perhaps a little better because of the word ecclesia in the New Testament, but I do not know whether it is such a good idea either. Surely there must be some way round it! Halford House was just the name of the house we met in and we were very thankful that we had that name. That helped us a little. People would say, "They are the folks at Halford House or the company at Halford."

Company is another word we often used referring to a company of believers.

Q:

Does the lack of elders hinder the church's growth or is it simply the lack of leadership, authority, responsibility.

A:

I hope from answering these questions it is quite clear that at the very beginning when you are only two or three, why bring up the question of leadership, eldership or anything else? All we need to do is love the Lord, love one another, care for the things of the Lord and His purpose, and be together. We pray and trust that from three we shall grow to six and from six to twelve and so continue on. Once we start to multiply and the numbers reach the forties, then the question of leadership and responsibility become quite clear. If there is not an emergence of some kind of responsibility taking place, then there will be a hindrance to that company. A company of forty people are not going to be able to come together without a number of brothers really taking responsibility. The whole thing would be so careless and loose. For example, who is going to decide when to meet, where to meet, and how to meet? If a problem comes up concerning the matter of discipline, who is going to exercise the discipline? Of course, having an enemy we will very quickly be destroyed. There is no doubt that the church's growth will be hindered once we have started to grow and multiply unless there is the emergence of leadership and authority in that company.

Q:

How should one encourage a brother who has a deep consciousness of self and a feeling that it has not been fully dealt with to serve and function in the church?

A:

I know a number of these brothers and I sometimes feel the best idea is to give them a good kick! However that is not the spiritual way to do it. I cannot help feeling that one of the big problems in leadership or functioning in any way in the church is unbelief. People, whom God has really dealt with in this matter of knowing in their spirit if they should be functioning, know that they have a part to play and they almost intuitively know what that part is; but then they get all tied up in knots. (Understand that I am not talking about this big-headed thing where someone has a great ministry).

I realize that some have made too much of this matter of the tree of the knowledge of evil and the tree of life so that it has almost become an error. But I have to say that the tree of the knowledge of good and evil does symbolize a kind of life in which we spend all our time weighing up the credits and the debits on any given situation, and the tree of life symbolizes a dependence and reliance upon the Lord. Our problem is that as soon as a person intuitively knows that they should be functioning in a certain way, they then switch to the tree of knowledge of good and evil and start to weigh up everything, saying, "Now, is it me? Is it the Spirit? This is on the credit side, this is on the debit side," so that they become totally paralyzed. That is what I mean by having living faith. If God really is leading you in a direction, you must step out in faith.

Now most of us can remember when we first prayed in public. We became worried and frightened and thought, "Is it the Spirit? Is it not the Spirit?" Ultimately you would have never burst forth in public had you not taken a step forward, opened your mouth, and made all the mess that first time. Is it not interesting that people can come into a prayer time and feel absolutely out of it and go away saying, "I did not feel a part of it." Yes, of course, because they never opened their mouth. Yet when we open our mouth and are part of it, immediately we feel we are "in."

So what do we do with this kind of person? I think we have to pray. It is one thing to have a deep consciousness of self and a feeling that it has not been fully dealt with; thank God for that. But does anyone ever feel that their self-life has been fully dealt with? I would like to meet them. The apostle Paul said he was the least of all saints at one point (Ephesians 3:8), but the last letter he wrote said he was the chief of all sinners (1 Timothy 4:15). So the nearer he got to the end and the fulfillment of the ministry, the more unworthy in one sense he felt. That, however, is not the point. This is where we need an anointing of the Spirit. I have no doubt about it at all. Otherwise brethren spend their whole time tied up in knots in a strait jacket sitting there debating whether or not they should be doing this or that. What they need is the Holy Spirit to come upon them and provide the dynamic by which they are, as it were, propelled into functioning. This matter is so important. So whoever has written this question (I have a funny feeling it could be a sister), pray for this brother that he may have an anointing.

One of the great functions of sisters is to pray for brethren that they would somehow have a spiritual bomb placed behind them to blow them forward into fulfillment of God's purpose for them. When the brothers fulfill their place, the sisters fulfill theirs. There is no truer thing than when the brothers really start to fulfill their function in the church, there is no need for Women's Lib; the women are liberated and they can start to fulfill their rightful place. When the men do not fulfill their place, the women get all tied up in knots, and sometimes they get into the wrong place or doing what they should not be doing.

Q:

Once someone has been placed in a position of leadership, such as being an elder or deacon, and after some time fails to fulfill the qualifications mentioned in 1 Timothy 3, for example, their children become unruly or drugs or fornication are involved, should they be removed? How? Should they be restored in time if the situation changes? Who should do the removing and restoring? Should it be handled publicly?

A:

Oh, dear! What a question! Well now first of all I must say straightway that it is a tragedy when brethren who are leaders fall into sin. But may I just say something about the matter of children first and foremost? Do not jump too quickly to judge a brother who is in the leadership who has a child or a couple of children that are at present proving very, very difficult. Be careful that when you judge you will not be also judged. I have heard many a person say something about a marriage that is going through a rocky period, perhaps some leader's marriage, and they have pontificated upon it and said how wrong it is and how the person should be removed, only to find a few years later that their own marriage has gone through a far worse period. Whatever judgment you mete out is liable to be the judgment you receive.

On the other hand, one of the most marvelous evidences that a man is in the right place is that something is happening in his family. This does not mean that there are not black sheep in the family. There will always be black sheep in any family. It does not mean that the children of those brethren will not kick over the traces, that they will not have a period of very real rebellion and may even go into the far country. This does not mean that a brother's responsibility of leadership is now ended and he is to be removed. Surely it means that we should rise up and pray for that brother and that family more than we have ever prayed before and support them in their time of trial. Because they are in the forefront, if the enemy can get that family he has really got something.

On the other hand, if a husband cannot rule his own household, how can he rule the church? When children answer back, when they literally show a public disregard, then I wonder should the man be in leadership. If he cannot lead his own family, can he lead the house of God? That is a different matter. Should the man have ever been there in the first place? We are not looking for copy book perfection. That is when people get the idea that leaders and their wives according to Timothy should be absolutely perfect, which is impossible. The apostle Paul has given us those things as a guide, if you like, to spiritual character.

Now what do we do when, God forbid, someone has fallen into sin or into drug taking or alcoholism? I am afraid in my experience that I have found such things have happened in leadership. Perhaps the most common is adultery. I have no question about it, the brother should be removed. First we must be absolutely sure that it is established in the mouth of two or three witnesses. We must never accept the witness of one person. There must always be two or three as we are told in the Scripture (II Corinthians 13:1). However, once established, then there should be a removing. This has to be done on the part of the church and the other brethren. Of course in the New Testament it would have been apostolic. Paul was writing to Timothy and telling him what to do on some of these very matters.

Q:

I am involved in a fellowship at school in which the Lord has blessed us with over a hundred members. There are several people involved in leadership at the fellowship but no formal leadership has been established. My question is: how should the leadership in such a group be organized if at all? Right now a group of us meet and make decisions by consensus. Also we have a problem in how to view ourselves, what needs should we try to meet, and what about doctrinal matters.

A:

First of all I will seek to answer the question on how you should view yourself. May I say quite clearly that a fellowship in a university, college or school is not a church. It is very important that we understand that because if we try to make it a church, we get into a mess. What then happens is when people begin to see things to do with the church they say, "Oh, now our fellowship must be the same as this." There are principles that may be the same but I would be clear that there is a difference.

A fellowship in a college or university is really a getting together of the believers in that place for fellowship. It cannot function in the way that the church ought to function, but it meets a particular and specific need on the part of believers in that college, university, hospital or whatever it is. So we view ourselves simply as a Christian-get-together, as a fellowship of believers for testimony, for outreach, and for support of one another in a way where we can understand each other. If there are folks in a hospital, they will understand each other better than people outside and they can help and pray for one another because they understand the problems that everyone is facing within that circle.

What about leadership? Obviously in a fellowship in a university or a college you cannot talk in the way that I have been talking about the emergence of leadership in the church because the church should be a settled matter. A fellowship, by its very nature, would have a changing population where all the time there are some coming in, some going out, new ones coming in, and old ones going out. Therefore you cannot think of it in those terms. You can have a recognized leadership if you like, as they often do in Britain or Europe, and in the Intervarsity Fellowship circles where there is a certain sort of way that they arrange and appoint leaders, I do not think there is anything particularly wrong with that. But it seems the way you are doing it at present is good. If there are a number of brothers there who meet together, who take responsibility and out of it there is a consensus of feeling before God as to the way it should be done, that is a very good way and it also teaches those young brothers to look to God and to read the mind of God by the Spirit which I believe is very important. Anything that teaches any of us how to distinguish the mind of God in prayer and in fellowship is invaluable.

Q:

I am used to the traditional understanding of calling being a personal sense of being led into ministry. Today when a man holds a full-time secular job, etc., how does one sense a calling? Is it personal? Is it others coming to you? How do you go ahead into a calling to either confirm it or test it?

A:

Now I hope I have understood this question correctly. Regarding a calling to ministry, to leadership or whatever, I do not think being full-time stops you from having a calling from God. Let me just insert that I am not at all sure we can call anything secular. You can be scrubbing a floor and it can be sacred. It is a question of whether you are sacred. If you are secular, then what you do is secular. But if you become sacred, then what you do is sacred. In other words, if you are sanctified, set apart for God, then what you do likewise marvelously comes within that sphere.

You can have a full-time job and yet God may give you a ministry of the Word in the company of believers in which you are found. He may have called you to that. There may then come a time when you will have to give up your ordinary job and give yourself entirely to the Lord in this matter. Some people say, "Well, should I not do that earlier?" No, do not ever do it until it is absolutely necessary. Charles Haddon Spurgeon, a man truly anointed of God, once said, "Never preach and never enter the ministry until you are forced to." This idea where people say, "Oh, God is calling me," means what? So what do you do? You go sit there and do nothing because there is nothing to do. So you are now called. Quite honestly I do not understand that kind of calling. It seems to mean that normally a person would be called to a ministry and then it slowly opens up. As they begin to fulfill it the demand becomes more and more until in the end they cannot fulfill that ministry and have a normal job alongside. When that occurs it is quite clear that they are going to have to give themselves to the ministry to which God has called them.

First of all I must point out that calling is personal in the first analysis. I am quite sure of that. I would be very worried if I were to suddenly get hold of a particular brother and say to him, "You are called to the ministry!" I have thus put a big idea into the poor brother's head whereby he thinks, "Oh! I have been called to the ministry!" He now goes round and round in circles sort of working up this ministry into which he has been called. Of course, it is nonsense, yet these things happen. Sadly I have been in so-called apostolic meetings where they designated that a certain brother marry a certain sister. Do you know they went and did it?! I do not believe in that kind of thing at all. I think it is monstrous.

I have no doubt that the first thing in a calling is a sense you yourself must have from the Spirit of God and then it should be confirmed in the church. In other words, there should be others who feel the same thing and when you share it, they say, "Brother, I feel that you are right in this but go carefully. Do not rush, wait back and test it." There are certain brothers I know for whom I have waited a year or two before they said that they had received this call, but once they acknowledged it there was no need to say "test it;" rather I have said, "Get on with it!" Go ahead with the Lord, do not wait.

Q:

Did you sense a personal calling in the ministry of the Word and if so how did it dawn on you?

A:

Dawn on me!? First let me repeat that it must be personal, because how the Lord dealt with me is not necessarily the way He would deal with someone else. I was less than thirteen years of age when the Lord first called me in a vision and I saw the Lord. I did not see His face, but I saw the Lord and He quite distinctly called me to a ministry, to a task. Then shortly afterward He confirmed it in three other ways. I was only a kid who came from a pagan background, so I did not know my Bible very well. Then I went to

Alan Redpath who was pastor at that time and he said, "You must get it confirmed by the Word," and I could not understand what he meant. It was during the war years and I thought a bomb would have to drop on us and I would be miraculously saved. That must be the confirmation you get for this kind of thing, I thought. But in actual fact, God gave me a number of Scriptures which have been the foundation of my entire ministry through the years.

The interesting thing is that the Lord called me when I was all flesh. What a risk the Lord takes when He calls us. I remember that when the Lord first visited me in such a miraculous way I was greatly humbled and wept very much. But I did seek the Lord. I was "one hundred percent" and ready to sacrifice anything, even in my flesh, and I did try to live the Christian life. Oh my, I did try! I spent hours in prayer, hours reading the Word, and I witnessed to somebody every day until I wore myself into a frazzle. Finally, in absolute desperation when I thought I would give up everything, the Holy Spirit came upon me. Then in that state of being at an absolute end I saw two things: The Holy Spirit was in me with authority from God the Father to reproduce the nature and life of the Lord Jesus. From that day to this I left the job to Him. Before I had always asked Him to help me to live the Christian life, but then I abdicated and said, "Well, now, dear Holy Spirit, You are here to do this and I will obey."

The second thing I saw was that I was crucified with Christ. When I saw that, it was a great relaxation. The façade I had and the projection of a Christian personality all fell away and I became myself. I never bothered about myself from that day to this. I just thought, "I am myself. God crucified me, He finished with me, and if there is anything of the Lord in me, well thank God for that, and that is what I trust will come through."

That is how I was called. So at the beginning it was all flesh. I cannot say the ministry began then, because it did not for years. In fact the very first time I ever ministered the Word I made such a mess of it I got the people in such laughter, not because I was being funny but because I became so tied up. I was unbelievably nervous. For two years I never opened my mouth. After two years I finally opened my mouth while I was in Egypt and they had to force me. The only way I would agree to it was to write down every word I was going to say. Only the people who were responsible for the meeting knew that I actually read what I said. But so many people were blessed, some got saved and they could not believe that I had read my message. I had been so afraid after that first experience that I had to write everything down.

Now I am not expecting anyone to follow that way which is rather unusual. But what I think is wonderful is that God does call us because He knows the end from the beginning. Therefore sometimes He calls us when we are in total flesh—saved but all flesh. Then He starts to deal with us, bringing us slowly but surely to an end of ourselves. I can actually trace the ministry that God has given to me in practical terms to the day that I saw the Holy Spirit was in me and upon me and that I was crucified with Christ. From then on I saw people saved without my straining or pushing and I saw other people helped and taught because it really was a releasing of a ministry of the Lord.

Q:

Brother Lance talked about responsibility in the body of Christ. He said if God has anointed you, that you are responsible for expressing the life within you and not repressing it, not burying your talent. How do you know if God has anointed you and how do you know if you are doing what God has asked you to do? Sometimes I am clear about what the Lord seems to be saying but I am too inhibited to say anything lest others disagree. I have run into this problem before and instead of expressing the life within, I repress it for fear of offending. So I say nothing now and am very discomforted inwardly because of it. I feel I am not functioning in the body and have become useless to the Lord. What shall I do?

A:

This is a good question. I am quite sure it finds an echo in many hearts, if I go by the questions I am personally asked.

First of all regarding anointing: How do you know if God has anointed you? I must say that in a spiritual experience you may not know at what point you entered in. For example, I know people who were converted who literally, coldly, took a step in faith and it was weeks and months before they really knew they were born again. But they took that step of faith. I know others who have taken a step over the question, for instance, of being crucified with Christ. They really saw it and in cold faith they committed themselves to the Lord and went forward. There was no great feeling. But I have to say that in the matter of anointing, generally speaking you know.

I do think temperament comes into this. If a person has a very phlegmatic-type of temperament—very level, very unemotional, someone who never cries—I think it is possible to have an experience of anointing where they might even wonder if they have received that anointing. The one thing about anointing is that even if the person anointed does not know they are anointed, everybody else does. People will go for miles to hear an anointed servant of the Lord. It is the difference between night and day, between someone who can take things of God and speak of things of God and someone who cannot. It is even the same in such a natural thing as playing the piano. When a man has an anointing you meet the Lord through their playing. You are not just left with beautiful playing; you actually have something ministered to you. It is the same with singing. I know people who sing and they dazzle me with their ability and I think they have beautiful voices and that is what I am left with. But other people sing and they leave me with the Lord. Something is ministered into my heart. Now that is the difference between someone un-anointed and someone anointed.

However, I would like to point out that Jesus was born of the Spirit, but when He was thirty years of age He was anointed with the Holy Spirit. Generally speaking, anointing is a distinct experience that we enter into after having been saved. It is to do with service and functioning. If we look at the history of the church, we will discover that all the men whom God has used have all had a real experience. I find it so interesting because there is such a wide variety of experience and a variety in the way that it has happened.

I knew Billy Graham before he had his experience and I could keep you in stitches of laughter over what happened before that experience. I shall never forget him preaching in London in Westminster Chapel and he was acting out the lions eating the Christians in the arena at Nehms. He was rolling around on the ground fighting with the lions and then in the end there was an appeal with soft blues-type music in the background and repeated appeals to come forward. Very few went forward on those occasions. I felt so sorry for him I almost wanted to go forward myself just to help him. I thought, "You have worked so hard, you poor man."

When he came back two years later you could hardly believe it was the same man. He stood there with his Bible open and it was the Word! The Word! The Word! When the appeal was given there was no music, but there was no need. He never appealed twice, but people poured forward. Later he said that in a retreat God had met him and knocked him out for nearly a whole day. He did not have to tell us this because it was perfectly apparent that something had happened whereby the Lord in him had been released in his ministry. Before it had been Billy Graham, now it was the Lord in Billy Graham. Now this is so in other ways. So I would say that generally speaking, considering most temperaments, you know when you are anointed.

This does not mean that you go round like a spiritual tank because now "you are anointed." This is not at all the case. When the anointing has come upon a person, I think they become very humbled. The Lord allows things to come our way to keep us very, very humble. The difference is that when we function there is a divine ability that was not there before.

Q:

How do you know if God has anointed you and how do you know if you are doing what God has asked you to do?

A:

Now that is a little more difficult. How do you know if you are doing what God has asked you to do? In some areas we know very well. I know that the Lord told me to go back to my own people, so I know that I have to live in Israel and I have to be an Israeli citizen, which I am. I know that I had to do that because God three times spoke to me about it. There are other areas in which I know and there are other times when I do not know. In the end I have had to take a step in faith and go forward. I am not absolutely one hundred percent certain that I should be involved in this meeting or involved in this conference, but I believe that the Lord has somehow not said no and so I will go forward in faith. I find sometimes that the Lord is more in those times than some of the other times in which I am quite clear that He has directed.

In this matter, I suppose this person is wondering if they have a function that they should be in. Let me point out that your brothers and sisters have good "horse sense" if you understand what I mean. When it really comes to it, you will find that the church itself and the leadership in the church will be more accurately able to tell you whether you are doing what God wants or not. There are a lot of people in the life of the church who are actually square pegs in round holes. They really are trying to do things. They have an idea that God has called them and it is ridiculous. All of us could tell them they are boring to a degree or what they do is always problem-producing because they are square pegs in round holes. If they would only be humble we could say to them: "Do you know what your gift is? It is that." In this way we could help one another to find what the Lord has given. So how do you know if you are doing what God wants? Sometimes God clearly tells you, but always the evidence that you are doing and functioning in the place that you ought to be is that the church is built up and blessed and they meet the Lord through your ministry, your functioning or whatever it is.

Q:

Now concerning the second part of the question: Sometimes I am clear about what the Lord seems to be saying but I am too inhibited to say anything lest others disagree. I have run into this problem before and instead of expressing the life within, I repress it for fear of offending.

A:

This is disgraceful! The reason I say it so harshly is because you must understand that this is disobedience. We must not play with this kind of thing and pat yourself on the back saying, "Very humble." You are not being humble at all, you are being disobedient. You have got to find the grace of God and the power of God to do what He wants you to do and you must not expect me or any other leader to comfort you in this kind of thing. It is quite wrong. You are holding back something God has given you for the church. If there is life within you which you should be expressing, yet for fear of others you are repressing it, you are burying your talent. I for one am not going to comfort you when the Lord says, "take away from him what he has and give it to another." I have to stand by my Master on this matter. We have great empathy for you because we have all been there ourselves; nevertheless, we should be hard on you. You need to repent and go to the Lord, and if you have not had an experience of the empowering of the Holy Spirit, that is what you need. This is not to throw your weight around in the church, but you need divine ability to distinguish when you should speak and when you should not.

Furthermore, you need deliverance from the fear of your brothers and sisters. This fear is a phantom. In some companies of believers there are ogres and ogresses; there is no doubt about that. There are some who put the fear of God into you in a quite wrong way because they know everything, they are very critical and they seem to judge everything that is said. But normally this feeling is a phantom. When you have given what you really have of the Lord, you will find the very people you were afraid of are the people most blessed. They are ready to thank you and very ready to open up.

Let me tell you a very funny story. I have a very dear friend in Finland and before he began to see more of the Lord he was a Lutheran pastor for years. There is one part of Finland that is Swedish-speaking and the people are very expressionless. Now the Finnish Fins are Asiatic people, and they express their feelings and are a little more volatile. But the Swedish-speaking Finns are much more mask-like and you never know what is going on behind their faces. You can speak for half an hour or an hour and you just do not know what is going on until all of a sudden you see someone weeping at the end. Then you know that something has touched them; otherwise you cannot not go by their faces.

This Lutheran pastor went to a certain place and began to preach. He had a sense of humor and was a very lively brother with a real ministry from the Lord. He began to speak and every time he had a service he noticed a sister sitting in a certain place with a face like thunder. After a while he found that he could not look anywhere else but at that sister. Whatever he said he would look back at her but she never smiled, never looked happy, and never looked open but always looked as though she thoroughly disapproved. She never said anything, but she always came to the service and left with never a flicker of warmth in her face.

After a year he began to have nightmares and in the night he used to see this sister's face and he would say, "My ministry is shriveling up." He became so afraid of this person. Then one day at the end of a service he saw her standing at the back. He thought, "Oh my goodness, the confrontation has come. She is now going to tell me how ungodly I am, how hopeless I am, what a terrible kind of ministry I have, and how unspiritual and superficial it is." But he braced himself and said, "However, I will go and seek to learn from this sister." So he went toward the back and she waited for him. When he was quite near to her she took two steps forward and said, "Pastor Loluch!" without a flicker, "I have sat under your ministry for two years and I cannot tell you what a blessing it has been." With that she turned and left. This dear sister had been a nightmare to this brother for all of those years, and he had no idea that she was being so blessed.

Now this is the way the enemy works on us. We have a terrible fear in our companies that somehow or other people do not agree. We believe they might jump on us and say, "It is flesh; it is not in the Spirit." It is phantom. We have all got it. We all feel it. It is something over which living faith has to be exercised. If God has given you something, you need the power to be able to do what is right at all times. Sometimes you do not realize that there are others there who are also fearful and when you break through and give what you have, they break through with what they have. So I hope this will help.

3.
A Living Sacrifice

Romans 12:1–8

I beseech you therefore, brethren, by the mercies of God, to present your bodies a living sacrifice, holy, acceptable to God, which is your spiritually intelligent worship. And be not fashioned according to this world: but be ye transformed by the renewing of your mind, and ye may prove what is the good and acceptable and perfect will of God. For I say, through the grace that was given me, to every man that is among you, not to think of himself more highly than he ought to think; but to think as to think soberly, according as God hath dealt to each man a measure of faith. For even as we have many members in one body, and all the members have not the same office: so we, who are many, are one body in Christ, and severally members one of another. And having gifts differing according to the grace that was given to us, whether prophecy, let us prophesy according to the proportion of our faith; or ministry, let us give

ourselves to our ministry; *him do it with liberality;*
or he that teacheth, to his *he that ruleth, with diligence;*
teaching; or he that exhorteth, to *he that showeth mercy,*
his exhorting: he that giveth, let *with cheerfulness.*

I find it quite a difficult thing to share on Christian leadership especially when we have had a number of these times, not only ones that I have been involved in but also with other brethren. There probably will not be a single thing I say that you have not heard before, and this fills me with a very great fear. The very fact that we have to say the same thing again and again is evidence of its importance. Yet at the same time it can be a very great danger. We think that because we are acquainted with truth that it is ours, and we fall into the trap which we find throughout Christendom of believing things that we never ever expect to become flesh and blood experience.

Leadership is Strategic

I have absolutely no doubt at all in my mind that all our troubles stem from our leadership. Leaders always like to talk about the flock—how apathetic the flock is, how indifferent the flock is, how impossible the flock is, how obstinate the flock is, the lack of appetite in the flock, the lack of spiritual character in the flock, and the lack of zeal and devotion in the flock. But I have never yet found any trouble with the flock. All the trouble is with the shepherds. The sheep find each other so naturally. I imagine that most of the sheep here in Richmond, England who are born of God would find each other very easily if it was not for the shepherds. They love each other. It is a natural spontaneous thing. They almost sense those who belong to the flock and it is like a natural gravitation to flow together. The problem is the leaders. I remember years ago a Divine in Britain saying, "Never bother with your front row where the leaders are; all the trouble is there. Speak over them to the flock because that is where the real value is."

Leadership is strategic, it is vital and it is of the utmost significance as far as God is concerned. He will go to any lengths to produce real leadership once He has a willing candidate. Therefore I want to underline three essential characteristics of leadership.

We have mentioned some of these things many times. So let's ask the Lord that He will really make our times together living to every one of us, as though we have never heard this before in our lives.

A Living Sacrifice

If I were asked what I thought was the most essential characteristic in leadership, I would unhesitatingly reply that it is this matter of being a living sacrifice. You cannot expect devotion in the flock if the leaders themselves are not an example of being a living sacrifice—not a dead sacrifice, but a living sacrifice.

It is so interesting that in this letter, which is one of the most tremendous in the whole Bible, after the apostle has surveyed the whole question of our salvation, our life in Christ and the church, he comes to this point:

I beseech you therefore, brethren, by the mercies of God, to present your bodies a living sacrifice, holy, acceptable to God, which is your spiritually [intelligent] worship" (Romans 12:1)

This word service or in the old version reasonable service is in fact best rendered spiritually intelligent worship. It is not a matter of a once only sudden dedication of your life in a moment of emotion. This is a cold-blooded decision on your part to lay down your life for the Lord, for His church and for the dying world around us. It is as if the apostle draws together all the strands which he has so amazingly interpreted and defined for us in the previous eleven chapters with this cry from his heart: "I therefore beseech you, brethren, that you present your bodies a living sacrifice, holy acceptable to God, which is your spiritually intelligent worship." God is not the least bit interested in a kind of sudden spurt of emotion where you suddenly say, "I will be everything for You, Lord! I will go anywhere for You, Lord!" Only within a week or two you find an exit, a fire escape from your dedication.

It is interesting that the apostle goes on to talk about the body of the Lord Jesus. This whole passage is about service and ministry. He says, "Through the grace that was given me, I say to every man that is among you, not to think of himself more highly than he ought to think" (Romans 12:3). In other words, do not have an exaggerated opinion of your function, your status in the body of Christ, or of your ministry, but think soberly, that is, be absolutely realistic. You ought to have a realistic evaluation of your place in the work of God and in the body of the Lord Jesus. He speaks of us being many members of one body in Christ, and with all these many gifts every one of us must seek to function as we ought to function.

But why do so few believers really function in the body of Christ? This is a problem in the companies, fellowships and assemblies that are represented here. Our problem is that there is a kind of nucleus that functions, but there is also a large amount of dead wood. We are not speaking of dead wood in a critical way because they are good sheep, but for some reason they are timid or inhibited or not really functioning. Something is wrong.

The Key to the Functioning of the Whole Body

The apostle puts his finger upon this question of being a living sacrifice as the key to the functioning of the whole body. It is the functioning of leadership which has as its calling the development of the ministries of the body and the bringing of the body to the place where it can build itself up in love. That is the whole point. It is not that we are to make the whole fellowship dependent upon us. Rather the whole aim of ministry, the whole aim of leadership, is to bring into being a fellowship that can build itself up, that can function powerfully, effectively, realistically, and spiritually. It is not knowledge, it is not even training. You can go to a theological seminary and emerge still not having anything like this. You can have a knowledge of the Bible whereby you can beautifully and soundly expound passage after passage, but you will not necessarily produce this. You may have had visions, but you will not necessarily produce this. You may have had revelations but you will not necessarily produce this. It is not the amount of revelations or the amount of visions that you have had, nor the amount of mysteries that you are acquainted with, nor the amount of knowledge that you have accumulated, nor the amount of training that you have received, nor even the amount of zeal that you possess; it is a question of whether you have finally, by the grace of God, fallen into the ground and died.

A Living Sacrifice Reproduces Life

A living sacrifice! Because we are so used to this phrase there is a kind of glamour about it: "Oh how wonderful to be a living sacrifice!" There is nothing lovely about being a living sacrifice. It is a place of blood, a place of being cut up, a place of being burnt, a place of fire and a place of smoke. I do not think there is anything very beautiful from one point of view about being a living sacrifice, but the results and the consequences of being a living sacrifice are wonderful in the extreme. For wherever people fall into the ground and die, life is reproduced in others. You can talk and instruct people until you are blue in the face, you can have meeting after meeting, you can have marvelous Bible studies, but it does not make the church any more effective. You cannot reproduce in another person the character that God has obtained in you by instructing them. What we often do is make awful imitations of ourselves.

Now if there must be one of me, it is best for there to be only one of me. It is a terrible thing when I try to instruct someone and somehow make them like me so that there are a whole lot of us all looking alike, acting alike, speaking alike, and serving the Lord alike. It is exactly what God does not want. What God wants is a reproduction. This is altogether a different thing and a different principle. Somehow God takes the spirit that is in me and the principles upon which I live and He transplants them into you so that they become yours in a totally original way; then you develop in an original way.

A Body Has to Be Born

This is the problem in the church. It is not just that we need instruction; God only knows that we need instruction. It is not that we just need training, God knows that we need training, but the problem is to reproduce in others the kind of life and character that alone can satisfy God. You cannot produce a body; it has to be born. You can put together a machine, and we only have to look at Christendom to see the number of machines that have not only been created in the past but are in the making today. Left to ourselves this is what we all do; we can do no other. We have to produce systems because somehow the easiest thing for us to do is to put together a machine. But how do you put together a body? You can have all the perfect members of a body and stitch them all together, but it is still a dead body. It will never function, it will never move, it will never think, it will never have the breath of life in it. Only by reproducing can that life that is in you grow in another so that you are reproduced in a family. That is what I believe is the true character of leadership.

Here Paul puts his finger on the whole matter by saying that the key to this body, which has many members functioning, yet is one body in Christ, with everyone fulfilling his place and part and everyone contributing, is that there have been those who have presented their bodies a living sacrifice, holy, acceptable to God. They have seen it as their spiritually intelligent worship. This is not kindergarten. This is spiritually adult. This is for those who are in the process of growing up in the Lord, who begin to discover that things are not as glamorous as they thought when they first entered into the work of the Lord, when everyone wants to be a leader. It does not take very long for us to get into leadership to find that we are looking around for ways of getting out of it! The fact of the matter is that the only way that God has ordained for the church to be born and the church to function is when you have men and women who can present their bodies a living sacrifice to God.

The Burnt Offering

In the Old Covenant there was the sin offering and the trespass offering. These two offerings were wholly to do with the question of sin, knowingly and unknowingly committed. That whole matter was covered by those offerings. But there was another offering that was far more important to which the sin offering and the trespass offering led and that was the burnt offering. And the burnt offering has something to do with service. It is as if God is saying, "The only way that I can do anything is when I have you as a living sacrifice." This is what the apostle is talking about—the burnt offering, a whole burnt offering, a living sacrifice, holy acceptable to God. This is spiritually intelligent worship.

We shall never recognize the will of God as good, acceptable and perfect unless we have a renewed mind. In other words, if we drop the façade which is part and parcel of fellowship and are totally honest with one another (which would be a dreadful shock and may not even be such a good idea), I doubt whether anyone would be able to say, "I have discovered that the will of God is good, acceptable and perfect." Most of us believe that the will of God is something to be endured with gritted teeth. It is something we can only face with Churchillian grit, having a fixed chin with a set mouth, a steely cold eye and a determination that declares, "We will do the will of God!"

Of course, we sing about the will of God being blessed and sweet, but when we get down to brass tacks who is ever going to state that, when in our heart we are frightened to death of the will of God? Most of us believe that the will of God is dreadful and have to be dragged into doing it. But of course we will not say that because we must be good Christians and smile at one another and say how good and perfect the will of God is.

Fashioned According to this World

We can never find the will of God good, acceptable and perfect if we are fashioned according to this world. That is the problem. After all we have to face the simple little fact that our spontaneous attitude is in keeping with how we have been fashioned according to this world. We were born this way. The very first thing we ever did when we were born was to "get." Our one cry before we could speak was "give me!" and from then on it has always been that we are naturally egocentric, self-centered creatures. The whole world revolves around us. As we grow up, if you are a husband, your wife and family center around you, and the church centers around you. If you are a wife, your husband and the children center round you. It is a natural thing. We are fashioned according to this world. Then we have the civil war of being born again. For when we are born again, into our being comes an altogether different principle, the self-less principle, the God-centered principle and suddenly we find within our being, right within ourselves, in our hearts, in our minds, a civil war. We are fashioned according to the world. In other words, our spontaneous reactions are selfish and self-centered. And even if we are sort of modest we want desperately that everybody recognizes it! It is something that is natural to us. We are fashioned according to this world and there is no way that you and I can find the will of God good, acceptable and perfect unless we have a renewed mind.

Concepts Govern Behavior

Now we are as we think. Everyone is the product of their thought. It is a very interesting thing that concepts govern behavior. In other words, your mind is a very important part of you, for as you think, so you are. That is the thing that determines in the end. You may believe in your heart a thousand things but it is your mind that determines your behavior and conduct and the way you live. And there is no way that you and I are going to be delivered from that except by a new mind, a renewed mind. In other words, we have to have a new outlook, a new attitude and a new mind, a renewed mind. What I just want to say very simply is this: you will never have that renewed, that consistent renewal of your mind so that you can do the will of God and find it to be good, acceptable and perfect unless you are a living sacrifice. There is no way. For the principle of this world is "I," first, second and last. A living sacrifice means that "I" has been crucified with Christ. It is another life and another mind.

What problems we have in Christian work today! Of course, they are not new, we have always had them. But when we really look at Christian work and especially Christian leadership, I have to tell you that I believe that many of us have been disillusioned; it is just another thing. God knows most of us get into this business of the work of God for wrong motives. If the Lord were not merciful there would not be any servants of the Lord. I do not know many who got into this business out of absolutely pure motives. They may have gotten into it because they really want to serve the Lord, but mixed up with serving the Lord is all this thing of becoming something, of becoming a power, of somehow or other being something. But there is only one answer to this whole thing—it is a living sacrifice. There is no other way.

Empire Builders

Then I want to say something about the real empire builders. Now when I say real empire builders, you see these little men in little fellowships who do not have the ability to be big empire builders, but they would like to be. Sometimes I find amongst us this kind of critical view as we look at certain ones—I wish I could mention names because it would be probably quite helpful but it would be quite wrong. But there are names that are household names to all of us. And we look down on them and say, "Oh, isn't it awful." I do not find it awful, I find it incredibly sad. Many of those men are real servants of God. They are born of God, they were saved by the grace of God and they were called by God into His work. And let me tell you something else, in their beginnings many of them were absolutely seemingly pure. They really gave themselves without reservation to the work of God—to preaching the Word, to evangelizing or whatever, and then because they never were aware of the motivating factors in their life, they were not aware of some of these energies in them, they began to build up something. It all seemed to be God, you see, and they began to build great premises and more and more, and before they knew where they were they had to finance the empire, and then came the crunch and they had to appeal and beg and beseech, "give, give, give." Earlier this year I watched on television a man that I knew many years ago in Britain and I knew him to be a true servant of God. I was so sad I could have wept as I saw this man on the television with a haggard face, and we saw all the magnificent buildings on the campus and all the works, and from beginning to end everything began and ended with money.

In Jewish things we have a story that originated somewhere in central Europe. The most famous story came from Prague, and it was about an old rabbi who made a puppet. He used to play with the puppet and gradually the puppet grew and grew until the puppet became a monster and took over the rabbi and everything to do with him. We call it in Jewish things the Golem. That is exactly what has happened in a lot of Christian work. It began as just a puppet without even realizing what were the motivating forces and images behind it and gradually it became a monster until in the end it is no longer serving the Lord. The thing they have created has become their master. And they are always carried along, hardly knowing where, by the thing they have created. This kind of thing is all in us. There is no key to this except presenting our bodies a living sacrifice. And you notice that the apostle does not say, "My dear brethren, I appeal to you to wait until suddenly one day something happens to you and you are blown along by a dynamic wind and power in the service of God." Now I believe in a baptism of the Spirit for service. I believe in a distinct experience of anointing for the service of God and I believe in power and in that tremendous breeze of the Spirit of God which alone can enable a man or a woman to do the will of God. But having said that, the apostle does not say, "Wait until somehow or other this great gale force hits you and takes you along." He says, "I beseech you therefore, brethren, by the mercies of God, to present your bodies a living sacrifice." You have to do something. It has to be a cold blooded decision on your part. And you will notice he does not say, "I beseech you therefore, brethren, by your knowledge of God, by the revelations of God, but by the mercies of God." In other words, there is not a person in this room who is not included in this. We can all by the mercies of God present our bodies a living sacrifice. That includes us all. It is a minimal thing. For there is not a person in the body of Christ, not a person in the kingdom of God, not a person in the family of God that is not there by the mercies of God. By the mercies of God we have been saved, by the mercies of God we have been indwelt by the Holy Spirit, and by the mercies of God we have been cared for by God. By those same mercies of God we can present our bodies a living sacrifice, holy, acceptable to God, which is your spiritually intelligent service.

The Grain of Wheat

The Lord Jesus put it in another way in words that all of you know very well: "Verily, verily, I say unto you, Except a grain of wheat fall into the earth and die, it abideth by itself alone; but if it die, it beareth much fruit. He that loveth his life loseth it; and he that hateth his life in this world shall keep it unto life eternal. If any man serve me, let him follow me; and where I am, there shall also my servant be: if any man serve me, him will the Father honor" (John 12:24–25).

That is a wonderful word. "If any man serve me, let him follow me and where I am there shall also my servant be." But the key is "Verily, verily I say unto you except a grain of wheat fall into the earth and die it abideth by itself alone." Now the word I want to underline is almost horrific. Listen: "it abideth by itself alone." I wonder whether that could be written as an epithet over much of our leadership. It abideth by itself—alone. In other words, it has never reproduced another. The key is this and Jesus said it: "Unless a grain of wheat fall into the earth and die, it abideth by itself alone. But if it die, it bringeth forth much fruit."

Now maybe you understand why I believe this matter of being a living sacrifice is perhaps the most essential characteristic of service. You can talk about knowledge, you can talk about visions, you can talk about power, you can talk about a thousand and one other things, but if a grain of wheat does not fall into the ground and die, it abides by itself alone! By itself alone. You can have all the experiences, and you can have all the visions and all the understanding, but if you do not know what it is to die, you will remain exactly what you are and who you are; there will be no others.

Now if that gets into your heart and my heart, perhaps it would bring a new complexion in our attitude to service. Maybe we would begin to cut back on the worthless. Maybe we would begin to say, "Well now, Lord, help me." Who can fall into the ground and die? It is impossible, isn't it? I was saying to them down in Clearwater at the other leadership time, I have always been haunted by that marvelous hymn, "O Love that Will not Let Me Go."

O love that wilt not let me go, I rest my weary soul in thee,
I give thee back the life I owe, that in thine ocean
depths its flow might richer, fuller be.

I get that; I have no problem with this, but it is the last verse that has always caught me:

O cross that liftest up my head, I dare not ask to fly
from thee, I lay in dust life's glory dead, and from the
ground there blossoms red, life that shall endless be.

It is this part: I lay in dust life's glory dead—that is the thing I find I cannot do of myself.

The Baptism of Jesus

I always found it an amazing thing that when Jesus came down into the waters of baptism to be baptized, John said that he saw heaven opened and heard the voice of the Father saying, "This is my beloved Son in whom I am well pleased." And the Holy Spirit came down upon Him in the form of a dove and abode upon Him. Now when I was first saved I used to hear many explanations of this and because I had never read the Bible, every time I read something like this I was very interested. The Christians always seemed to be so used to it that nobody even asked why the Holy Spirit came like a dove because they were all used to the symbol of the Holy Spirit being a dove. But I thought it was the most incredible or to be honest I thought it was a bit stupid. I mean wouldn't it be strange that the Holy Spirit came upon Him like a dove? I got the most incredible explanations. I was told the dove is gentle and pure. And I have no doubt, as the hymn says, that Jesus is "gentle, meek and mild," but it did not seem to have that effect on Him because He went out to the desert and had a colossal confrontation with Satan immediately!

It was years before I understood why the Holy Spirit came upon Him in the form of a dove. Jesus was born of the Spirit, but when He was thirty years of age, at the Levitical age when you enter into actual service, heaven opened and the Holy Spirit came upon Him in the form of a dove. It was years later I understood it. Why was Jesus baptized? I heard people say, "So that you and I should be baptized." I thought well that is an extraordinary thing; "Did He need to be baptized?" "No, no, He did not need to be baptized." "Well then why was He baptized?" "In order that you might know that you should be baptized." Well that seemed to me again rather strange. Because Jesus had no sin to wash away, no sin to confess, why did He have to go down into those murky dirty waters of the River Jordan and be immersed in them by John the Baptist? Quite rightly John said, "I should not be baptizing You; You should be baptizing me." But Jesus said, "Suffer it, that all righteousness may be fulfilled."

The Jordan River

It was only years later that I understood it. Those waters of Jordan represented Calvary three and a half years before He came to it. And it was as if heaven stood back and God said to the angels, "Don't give Him any help at all; let Him be absolutely alone in this. He as a man has to make a decision now as to whether He is going to choose the way of the cross or reject it." The heavens did not open when Jesus was on the bank. The heavens did not open when Jesus was in the water. The heavens only opened when Jesus went down into the water as if He said, "Father, I give myself to Calvary three and half years before it comes to pass. I will die daily for three and half years." And it was then that heaven opened and God said, "My Son in whom I am well pleased!" As if He was saying, "Like Father, like Son, this is my Son! He is like Me! He has committed Himself to the cross." And the Holy Spirit came down in the form of a dove. Why a dove? Because if you were a very wealthy Jew you brought a bullock or a heifer as your sin offering. And if you were middle class you brought a lamb or a ram. But if you belonged to the vast working class of the land who were so poor that they could hardly rub two pennies together, you brought two doves. And the moment John the Baptist saw the Holy Spirit come down in the form of one of those doves, he got it! And he said, "Behold, the Lamb of God who beareth away the sins of the world." John knew instantly that that sign of a dove was that Jesus was going to be a living sacrifice for the sin of the world.

How Can We Endure the Cross?

If the Lord Jesus needed the Holy Spirit in order to die daily, He Who was without sin, perfect in every way, He Who was without sin needed the Holy Spirit to enable Him to fall into the ground and die, in order for Him to die daily, to endure the gainsaying contradiction of sinners, to put up with the deprivation of difficult circumstances and situations, to put up with the antagonism of wickedness of an evil ecclesiastical mafia, how much more do you and I need the Holy Spirit. Be careful of talking about the cross without the Holy Spirit; it is nonsense. When people talk about the cross beginning first and last: "It is the cross, it is the cross, it is the cross," what does it do? It produces an inhibited, intimidated, darkened, heavy people. Oh! They are so dark. All they can think about is how great it is to be afflicted.

You know that is not what the Bible talks about. The Bible talks about going the way of the cross by the power of the Holy Spirit. People say to me that we should love the way of the cross. I have never heard such nonsense in my life. Anyone who talks about loving the way of the cross has never walked the way of the cross. It is impossible to love the way of the cross! That is sentimental trite. Jesus endured the cross for the joy that was set before Him.

It is the only way. It is for what is set before us that we go the way of the cross. To fall into the ground and die cannot be joy in itself. To be dismembered by other believers cannot be joy in itself. To become a doormat for everyone to trample over cannot be joy in itself. What kind of people are we? It is amazing to me the Gentile background Christians who have a kind of morbidity and misery that they sort of feel is very much part of being a Christian. If you laugh too much their attitude toward you is that you need to be delivered. They forget the wonderful word that says the ransomed of the Lord shall return to Zion with singing and with laughter in their mouths (Isaiah 51:11). If you are going the way of the cross, you need to laugh. I mean it. If you know anything about the cross you need to laugh. You will never get through otherwise; I tell you that from bitter experience. We need to be able to have the laughter of faith, that however terrible the way we are going, we are on the victory side and this way is leading us to the throne. It is the only way.

I call this an essential characteristic of leadership. It is not just a thought: "Well, it is necessary if you want to be reasonably effective in leadership." This is an essential, fundamental characteristic of leadership. It is a tragedy that in the flock there are more people who are living sacrifices than in the leadership. How can we shepherd someone who is a better living sacrifice than myself? I feel like sitting down and saying, "Sheep, shepherd me!" Oh, we are so stupid, as if the shepherd is anything in himself at all. None of us can be in this business but by the grace of God. Thank God He is doing something with us and if He does not have you now, He will. He will get you in the end by hook or by crook or by staff or rod. But the fact of the matter is that you and I need to face this simple little thing.

A Sentence of Death

The apostle puts it all in that marvelous II Corinthian letter which is all to do with service and he puts it like this: "Yea, we ourselves have had the sentence of death within ourselves, that we should not trust in ourselves, but in God who raiseth the dead: who delivered us out of so great a death, and will deliver us" (II Corinthians 1:9–10a). I cannot imagine it is a very nice thing to have a sentence of death. We normally do not throw a banquet because we have received a sentence of death. It is normally a rather horrifying thing. One good thing about a sentence of death is you do not have to worry anymore about leaking pipes, leaking roofs, unruly children or difficult circumstances. All that is over; you have a sentence of death within yourself, but he explains it even further: "That we are sufficient of ourselves, to account anything as from ourselves; but our sufficiency is from God; who also made us sufficient as ministers of a new covenant; not of the letter, but of the spirit: for the letter killeth, but the spirit giveth life" (II Corinthians 3:5–6).

A Treasure in Earthen Vessels

Let me repeat the phrase: ministers of a new covenant, not of the letter but of the Spirit. He then continues: "Therefore seeing we have this ministry, even as we obtained mercy, we faint not. For we preach not ourselves, but Christ Jesus as Lord, and ourselves as your servants for Jesus' sake. But we have this treasure in earthen vessels, that the exceeding greatness of the power may be of God, and not from ourselves; we are pressed on every side, yet not straitened; perplexed, yet not unto despair; pursued, yet not forsaken; smitten down, yet not destroyed; always bearing about in the body the dying of Jesus, that the life also of Jesus may be manifested in our body. For we who live are always delivered unto death for Jesus' sake, that the life also of Jesus may be manifested in our mortal flesh. So then death worketh in us, but life in you" (II Corinthians 4:1, 5, 7–12).

These chapters, headings and verses sometimes break up our whole understanding of something. It is all about ministry and leadership and functioning as sons of God. And he says, "Listen! This is the secret. We have this treasure in earthen vessels that the exceeding greatness of the power may be of God and not from ourselves." Now listen to the catalogue: "Pressed on every side, perplexed, pursued, smitten down." I am afraid that most of us if we heard such a catalogue being given by some servant of the Lord would say, "You are a candidate for a deliverance ministry. You need deliverance, brother. We send men like you to theological seminaries and Bible schools so that we may not be perplexed, let alone you. And here you are standing up there and saying, 'Pressed on every side, perplexed, pursued. Pursued?! By demonic things? Smitten down!?! Smitten down! When God wants you to stand up? What kind of servant of God are you?'"

We have this treasure in earthen vessels that the exceeding greatness of the power may be of God and not from ourselves. We are pressed on every side, yet not limited. Think of that. Perplexed, yet not unto despair. Pursued, yet not forsaken.

Smitten down, but not destroyed. Always bearing about in the body the dying of Jesus that the life also of Jesus may be manifested in our mortal bodies. Not just in our spirit, in our mortal bodies. Always bearing about in the body the dying of Jesus that the life also of Jesus may be manifested in our mortal bodies for we who live are always delivered unto death for Jesus' sake. Someone says, "Well, how can I?" You present your body a living sacrifice, God will take care of everything else. You do not have to worry.

Delivered unto Death

I love the word "always delivered." It does not say, "I deliver myself." I take the decision, I give up all right to myself, I take up my cross, I present my body as a living sacrifice, and God does the rest. Do you know who often does the delivering? Your brothers and sisters. They are always delivering us unto death for Jesus' sake. We get so angry with them. Sometimes the flock does it to leaders. There is a marvelous capacity of the flock for delivering servants of God unto death for Jesus' sake. And we get so angry. You know it needs the Holy Spirit to remind us, "But didn't you say that you wanted to take up your cross and follow the Lord Jesus?" "Yes," we say, "of course, but not like this! It is one thing for evil men to get at us, but it is another thing for the saints to get at us." God only knows how He can reach you. Sometimes the only way He can get to some of us is through the saints. But you will always be delivered.

Life Out of Death

Sometimes it is circumstances or situations that God arranges. He is a master at it. But I do not know what it is about all of us, but we have this lovely idea that this dying is going to be such a lovely thing, such a sort of spiritual kind of feeling, an ecstasy. It is not; the dying can be grim. But the answer of the apostle is very simple: "so then death worketh in us but life in you." That is spiritual adulthood. When we were babies, we wanted everything for ourselves. When we became children, discipline began, when we became adolescents, we went through the awkward stage, but when we reach adulthood, we had to learn to live for others. And so this question of service comes back to this matter of being a living sacrifice unto God. "I beseech you therefore, brethren, by the mercies of God, that you present your bodies a living sacrifice, holy acceptable to God, which is your spiritually [intelligent] worship. And be not fashioned according to this world: but be ye transformed by the renewing of your mind." You will never be transformed unless something happens to your mind. "And be ye transformed by the renewing of your mind, that you may prove what is the good and acceptable and perfect will of God." I dare to say that if every one of us were to become living sacrifices in this way, something would happen in a whole lot of fellowships and assemblies, something that may never have happened before. What teaching could not do, what instruction could not do, what conferences could not do, what experiences could not do, you will discover has happened through being a living sacrifice unto God. May God help us.

Shall we pray:

Dear Lord we have all heard this kind of message many times in one way or another through different lips, different tongues, perhaps even different emphases, but we have heard the truth again and again. Lord, we pray tonight that Your Holy Spirit will get it into our hearts. Write it in our hearts, Lord. May we really wake up to this issue. We begin to see that there is no way through unless service is going to be something for Yourself, something through which You can come, something through which Your will can be fulfilled, something by which You can work Your works, something through which the gospel of the kingdom could be preached in every nation for a testimony, something through which the body of Christ may be built up, and the bride make herself ready for the coming of the Bridegroom. Lord, only You can do this. Get it into our hearts, not as a mentally understood truth, but as a living truth revealed by Your Spirit. Lord, get it into our hearts in the way only You can do it for every one of us. And we ask it in the name of our Lord Jesus. Amen.

4.
Hearing the Voice of God

Revelation 2:1, 7

To the angel of the church in Ephesus write: He that hath an ear, let him hear what the Spirit saith to the churches.

Revelation 2:8, 11

And to the angel of the church in Smyrna write: He that hath an ear, let him hear what the Spirit saith to the churches.

Revelation 2:12, 17

And to the angel of the church in Pergamum write: He that hath

an ear, let him hear what the Spirit saith to the churches.

Revelation 2:18, 29

And to the angel of the church in Thyatira write: He that hath an ear, let him hear what the Spirit saith to the churches.

Revelation 3:1, 6

And to the angel of the church in Sardis write: He that hath an ear, let him hear what the Spirit saith to the churches.

Revelation 3:7, 13

And to the angel of the church in Philadelphia write: He that hath an ear, let him hear what the Spirit saith to the churches.

Revelation 3:14, 22

And to the angel of the church in Laodicea write: He that hath an ear, let him hear what the Spirit saith to the churches.

Revelation 13:17

And the Spirit and the bride say, Come. And he that heareth, let him say, Come. And he that is athirst, let him come: he that will, let him take the water of life freely.

John 10:3, 27

To him the porter openeth; and the sheep hear his voice: and he calleth his own sheep by name, and leadeth them out... My sheep hear my voice, and I know them, and they follow me.

Shall we just bow together in a word of prayer:

Heavenly Father, we want again to ask that You will presence Yourself in our time together that we shall meet with You and we shall hear Your voice. We pray Lord, that You will help us because so many of these things are things we have heard; but we pray that You will get them into our heart so that perhaps for the first time we hear in our spirit what You are saying. Dear Lord, we pray that You will wake us up to the days in which we are living that we may be those who are able to take responsibility, able to lead Your people, able to serve Your purpose and council in our own generation.

Lord, help us then as we commit ourselves to You. We thank You for the anointing which is ours through the finished work of our Lord Jesus, and we would by faith just take that anointing, grace and power for both the speaking and the hearing. Lord, let Your will be done in this time and may the result and consequence be something very precious to Yourself. We ask it in the name of our Lord Jesus. Amen.

Passing into the Last Era of World History

I want to cover yet another essential and fundamental characteristic in true leadership which I believe God really looks for in service. I have no doubt that we are moving progressively into the last period of world history for however long that lasts. It may last a century, two centuries, perhaps only a year, or maybe a decade, we just do not know. There are those who believe we are the last generation, but I have for a long time suspected that they are going to get us into a very big problem. They base it on the words of the Lord Jesus "this generation shall not pass away until all these things be fulfilled," and they link that with the fig tree coming into leaf (Matthew 24:32–34). If that is the case and a biblical generation is approximately forty years, then by 1988 the Lord Jesus has to return, give or take a few years, which means He might come in the next couple of years.

Gratton Guinness could say this in 1860–1870, and it was exciting, thrilling and challenging. Even in the earlier part of this century people could say it and it could also be said in the Second World War. I remember when I first found the Lord and I was so excited to hear that we might well be the last generation. But our problem is that whereas all these people could state these things then, the fact now is that we have very few years left if that theory is correct. It also means that we can determine exactly what the Lord Jesus said we cannot determine (which he said in the same breath). In Matthew 24:34, He said, "This generation shall not pass away until all these things be fulfilled," and He continued in verse 36 by saying, "But of that day and hour no one knows, not even the angels of the heavens, but my Father alone." Of course, it is obvious that if it is this generation we are in for trouble because we can now determine with every passing month more accurately when our Lord is going to come.

I therefore have for a long time suspected that this is a mistranslation. Years ago I asked a brother who was a great classical Greek scholar at Cambridge if he would look into the matter. He went away and a few days later he returned saying, "This word translated generation is an incredibly interesting word. It is a genetic name; in other words, it has a family of meanings. It is not just a word you can translate with only one English idea. It comes from a Greek root meaning to beget and one could say this begetting shall not pass away. It could mean, for instance, this family, that is, all those born of the same parentage; or this clan, all those born out of the same patriarch; or this tribe, all those born out of the same progenitors; or this race, all those who have the same source; or it can be this generation, all those born at the same time or at the same source of time. For some reason, the 1611 translators translated it this generation and every successive translation has continued with that word." But it is interesting that for the first time in the New International Version there is an alternative in the margin: "This race shall not pass away until all these things be fulfilled." I personally believe that is the real meaning of the words of the Lord. He was referring to the fig tree as the Jewish people. This race of people will not pass away although you are going to see them judged, dispersed and everything else, but this race will not pass away until all these things be fulfilled.

Now that means we have passed into the last era of world history. It could last a century or two centuries, which is very unlikely in my estimation. It could last just a few years, ten years, or twenty years, we do not really know, but we have passed into the last era of world history. If you will permit me to make this observation, I believe that the United States has been granted a further four years with a Christian president. It must be a long time since the issues in an election were quite as clear as they were in this last election. I think it would have been a judgment of God upon the American people if Mr. Reagan had not been elected, which means that you have a four year period with a man, whatever his faults might be, who really is a man who fears and honors God. In this sense it seems that the whole American people are given a further opportunity or a further chance, if I could so use the word, to seize the grace of God and move more deeply into the way of the Lord for these times. In particular, therefore, the reason I have said all this is because I believe leadership is vital. It is strategic in this matter.

The Key to a Whole Universe

Although not everybody is a leader, I believe that everyone wants in some way to serve the Lord. We want to be servants of the Lord. After all, every member of the body of Christ ought to be a servant of the Lord in some capacity. Every one of us ought to be taking responsibility. Therefore this matter of being a living sacrifice is all important. It is the key to a whole universe spiritually. That universe of understanding, of intimacy with the Lord, of wisdom applied, of power to serve God and to do His will all stem from being a living sacrifice consistently and in practice. If you only know it mentally and you are not a living sacrifice, that whole spiritual universe is closed. It is as if there is a closed heaven over us; it is not open. God never opens His heaven to the egocentric. He will save us because He loves us, but He will never bring us into that universal understanding, that universal intimacy, that universal practical union and communion with Himself until we become living sacrifices.

Hearing the Lord

The second essential characteristic of spiritual leadership which I believe to be a priority is the question of hearing the Lord. That must seem like kindergarten, but this matter of really hearing the Lord is strategic. It has to be a fundamental and essential characteristic of the servant of the Lord. One of the things that continues to amaze me wherever I go throughout the world is that so many people have a problem of hearing the Lord. I suppose one is asked more questions about how to know the will of God, how to know what the will of God is for an individual, and how to really know what God is saying, than any other area. If I may say so, men in particular have much more of a problem in this area than women. I do not know why this is; perhaps it is because they have learned to listen to their husbands, but women seem to have a more natural propensity for quite spontaneously hearing. They do not seem to have the same problem that the men folk have. But men seem to have a colossal problem in this matter. For instance, many servants of the Lord have actually told me that they have never heard the Lord in their lives. These are men who really, in many ways, would account to be something in the service of God. But they say, "I do not think I have ever really heard the Lord."

In my estimation, every born again child of God has heard the Lord. Men get tied up because they are perhaps waiting to hear an audible voice or something quite sensational and remarkable. Having a slightly more analytical type of mind, they tend to analyze it: "Is that the Lord?" It is almost impossible for the Lord to say anything to them because they would tear it to shreds the moment He says something. "Now, could that be my wife saying something? Or could that be brother so-and-so saying something? Or could that be my own voice saying something? Or could it be the world? Or could it be a demon?" In other words the moment the Lord says anything, the whole process starts—dissecting, analyzing, putting it under the microscope, and inspecting it as to whether it really is the Lord. Then of course, nothing ever gets done. While we are analyzing the whole thing the moment of opportunity to do the will of God is past forever. Then the Lord, in His grace, has to come back and shout again, only to be faced with the same problem. The more He shouts or speaks, the more dissection and analysis takes place.

The Birthright of the Child of God

This question of hearing the Lord speaking to every man or woman is the birthright of every child of God. Once, when I was speaking of this matter I said, "Of course, we have to be very careful of audible voices." And someone got hold of me and said, "I think I heard the Lord once audibly." I myself have heard the Lord audibly, but we do have to be careful of an audible voice because very often it can be demonic. Hearing an audible voice is not the problem. Some people may have a problem regarding that: "I have never heard an actual human voice saying, 'do this, do that; go here, go there.'" The point is that in your spirit you have a spiritual receiver and God or the Spirit of God can transmit and communicate with you. It is not that you actually hear an audible voice; it is that you receive the communication.

In Revelation the Lord said again and again, he that has an ear, indicating that even if one of your ears is deaf and you only have one functioning ear, then hear! The Lord was not being sarcastic because earlier when He was physically speaking to people, He said, "He who has ears (plural) to hear let him hear" (Mark 4:9). But when it had passed into another realm altogether of life in Christ, of being born again by the Spirit, He says, "he that hath an ear"—in other words, he that has the ability in his spirit to hear what the Spirit is saying. The Spirit does not have a mouth, He does not have a tongue, He does not have those physical things to be able to actually speak like you and me, but the Holy Spirit speaks. He communicates, and in your spirit you have the spiritual apparatus to receive the communications of God. Therefore every child of God in his or her spirit has the ability to hear and to understand what the Lord is saying, what the Spirit is saying, at any given moment.

This whole matter is of tremendous importance. No wonder the enemy has launched and set up such an onslaught over this matter of hearing what the Lord is saying. You can read the Bible and not hear. You can hear a message given in the power of the Holy Spirit and not hear what the Lord is saying. The Lord can be speaking to a whole company of people and you may be completely unaware of the fact that the Lord is speaking. Oh, how often in the history of the church God has spoken so clearly! The Spirit has been saying something to the churches in that day and it has been completely ignored and bypassed, as if He was not saying a single thing. This explains again and again why whole movements of the Spirit of God have died or become formalized or become something other than what God originally intended. So this matter is of tremendous importance.

Forgive me if this sounds like Sunday school, but we who are leaders and we who are servants of God need to hear this. The tragedy is that in the flock there are those who really hear the Lord and often the leaders do not. In other words, the tail wags the dog. All the direction comes from the rear because simple saints are clearer as to what the Lord is saying and what He wants than the leadership. This is quite ridiculous in one way. It is not that God always wants the leadership to be abundantly clear. It has been a humbling experience to find again and again that after having sought the Lord for a long time about a matter and with other brethren, some simple little old sister, whom you would think had nothing in her head, can hardly speak the Queen's English, comes up and very nervously says, "I wonder—

pardon me saying so—I just wonder whether the Lord might be saying this;" and then she says it. Then you say, "How come she got that?!" It seems that sometimes the Lord keeps us who are leaders very humble indeed by giving light to those who are not the more prominent members of the body. This brings the whole body into a oneness and a unity. But when every time anything happens, the direction comes from some unknown members of the body and the leaders are forever dull, then I wonder what is happening. Something is wrong somewhere and we need to attend to this matter. Why? Because you cannot do the will of God if you do not hear the Lord. It is as simple as that.

Doing God's Will

The most important thing in this day and age into which we are moving, this era of world history in which we find ourselves, is to do the will of God. There are a million things we could be panicked into doing in the days which lie ahead. We might go here and we may go there. Even the Lord said, "If they tell you he is in the wilderness, do not go there, if they tell you he is on the mountain, do not go there; if they tell you he is in the inner chambers do not go there!" (Matthew 24:26, author's paraphrase). You will know. But if you and I do not know how to hear the Lord, how can we do the will of God? The weaknesses which could have been masked in the day of affluence, prosperity and peace will be exposed when it comes to great strife and great problems. So we have time now in which to learn to hear the voice of God. Jesus, speaking about the shepherd, put it very simply: "To him the porter openeth; and the sheep hear his voice: and he calleth his own sheep by name, and leadeth them out. When he hath put forth all his own, he goeth before them, and the sheep follow him: *for they know his voice.* And a stranger will they not follow, but will flee from him: for they know not the voice of strangers" (John 10:3–5, author's emphasis).

I come from a part of the world in which there are a lot of sheep. I was brought up in Britain where there are millions of sheep and I now live in another part of the world where there are sheep and goats everywhere all mixed together. It has never ceased to amaze me that whenever you went into a field and the sheep were perfectly happy, if you talked to them they shied off. But in another part of the world some little Bedouin boy comes and says a few words, and all the sheep come immediately. If I were to go and stand there saying a few words, even aping exactly what he is saying, they would all run in the opposite direction. He says a few words and they come immediately.

Tending the Sheep

Sheep are not only very silly creatures, but they are also given to much disease. People have a sentimental picture of shepherds who love their sheep and sort of stroke each one every night before tucking them in bed. The idea portrayed is: "What a lovely picture of the Lord and His own." But in actual fact as I was once told by a shepherd: "We have a lot to do with the sheep because they can develop disease overnight. Foot rot can literally develop within twenty-four hours. Sometimes there can be an abscess or an ulcer that develops in the skin under the wool and therefore the shepherd has to inspect his sheep at least once every forty-eight hours whereas the goats can be left anywhere up to two weeks. Goats tend to be disease free and are quite intelligent. They can be left for quite a while but the sheep cannot. So the shepherd gets to know the weaknesses of individual sheep. He knows if a particular sheep might be given to foot rot or if a particular sheep tends to be prone to some other kind of illness. He gets to know his sheep by name and each sheep means something to him.

Once when I was in the Sinai there were masses of sheep from a whole number of flocks waiting to be watered. Among them was a Bedouin shepherdess with her whole flock of about one hundred sheep and goats, all black and white and all jostling with each other. I looked at them all and they seemed to be exactly the same. But all of a sudden I saw her look very intently into the midst of this seething mass. She then stooped down, took up a shallow pebble and aimed it with the most amazing accuracy at one particular sheep in the center of the whole flock which jumped up into the air when the stone reached its target and fled off into another flock. To this day I wonder how in the world she knew that sheep was not hers, for to me it looked precisely like the other ninety-nine. But she knew. These animals did not have a mark like those in Britain where they mark them with green, red or purple dye so the flocks can be differentiated. These sheep were not marked at all. But she knew that that particular one in that large flock was not hers. She knew it from a careful intimate relationship to each member of the flock. Those sheep knew their shepherdess' voice and she knew them. Jesus said, "My sheep hear my voice and I know them and they follow me" (John 10:27).

Now the interesting thing, especially with many men, is that they have this exact problem. They say, "How do I know it is not the voice of a stranger?" Jesus put it very succinctly and lucidly. He said, "They will not follow a stranger, for they know not the voice of a stranger" (John 10:5). Now Jesus is right and you are wrong. In your heart of hearts, if you will lay your analytical mind on one side for a moment, you know very well when it is the Lord and when it is not. We all know the voice of God; we just have to learn to hear Him and follow Him. But this matter of doing the will of God is a matter of hearing. Nobody can do the will of God who does not hear the voice of God.

It is interesting that it says, "Let him that hath an ear hear what the Spirit is saying to the churches" (Revelation 2 and 3). In other words the Holy Spirit may be saying something at a particular time to churches. What He said to those churches is very important for the whole of the history of the church, but it is also true that at different times the Holy Spirit is saying something to the churches in our day and generation. We really need to have the kind of listening ear that knows what He is saying to the churches and the way that He is leading us in our day and generation. This is very important if we are not to be led astray by thieves and robbers.

Thieves and Robbers

Jesus went on and said, "The thief cometh not, but that he may steal, and kill, and destroy: I came that they may have life, and may have it abundantly" (John 10:10). Now the problem with not hearing the voice of God and not doing the will of God is that the thief comes. Then there is a stealing, a killing, and a destruction of the flock. The stealing may be spoliation, or in other words, oppression comes. Something is lost, the meetings become heavy, we do not move with God in the way that we were moving with Him and we are not moving in the life of God in the way we had been. Everything becomes systematized and heavy, even in the freest meetings. Do not think that because we do not have a liturgy and we have the kind of free meeting where everyone can take part that we do not have a pattern. Some of our assemblies and fellowships have a more liturgical and rigid pattern than institutional places, and that is why the Holy Spirit sometimes finds it easier to work in some of those places than amongst us! This is because in the most institutional areas He sometimes finds an open door to burst out in life in a new way.

We need to be able to follow the Lord and hear what He is saying. This whole matter is extremely important and so we need to develop that hearing ear when God is saying something to us as a people. When we become dull, when we get spoiled, something is taken away from us and the livingness of our fellowship, the power of the Lord in our midst, the wonders and signs that God did, all disappear. A thief has come, and he has stolen. What has happened? The shepherds have deserted the flock and a thief has come in and spoiled; he has stolen.

Killing is individual. It is very sad in our fellowships and assemblies when those who ran well are killed. It is not that they actually die out; it is that they are killed as far as the purpose of God is concerned for the building up of the body of the Lord Jesus. They are disillusioned, disappointed, and somehow they have been tripped up by the enemy. The purpose of God for them to be a functioning part in the body of Christ, of the church, has been killed. Why? Because the shepherd is not doing his job. Something needed to be explained, something needed to be communicated. Perhaps a weakness at the very beginning sometimes known by the shepherds has never been communicated to that person and they have been unaware of it until the enemy blew it up into an area where he was able to kill the purpose of God for them in that particular part of the body. Furthermore, the destruction is not just a personal thing but is probably the destruction of a whole company. When we look into the history of God's work, so many assemblies and companies have come together and really functioned in the life and power of God and according to the will of God, but today they are no more. They are destroyed. The thief has come to steal, to kill and to destroy.

What is the purpose of Jesus? It is that "they might have life and that they might have life more abundantly." In other words the whole purpose of the Chief Shepherd is that the flock may be kept in eternal, overflowing and abounding life. Therefore every under shepherd has got to be someone who can hear the Lord. The voice of God is not only a warning; the voice of God is encouraging. We sometimes think the only time the Lord ever speaks is when He has something to warn us about. But in actual fact the vast majority of what God has to say is encouraging, exhorting, comforting, and strengthening. We need to hear the voice of God in this way.

The Servant Needs a Hearing Ear

If I may take this one step further, it is very interesting that the one necessity of a real servant is to have a hearing ear. In the days when people had servants, what point was there in hiring a servant if they could not hear what the master or mistress said? They did their own thing, in their own way and in their own time; that is not service. What I am saying is that if you want to be a good servant, the one important thing is hearing. It is no good hiring a deaf servant, for if you suddenly said to him: "We have five people coming to lunch," they cannot hear and will continue cleaning the silver. Then you raise your voice, "I said we have five people coming to lunch!!" The guests may come to lunch but the silver is still being cleaned. What is the point of having a servant like that? But the work of God is filled with such servants! The Lord is saying, "Such and such is going to happen!" and they go on cleaning the silver. It is service done at their own time, in their own manner and according to their own concepts. This is not service.

It is very interesting that the four gospels reveal the Lord Jesus in different ways. Matthew reveals Him as King; Luke as Man; John as God; and Mark as Servant. When John is used by the Spirit of God to interpret the Lord Jesus as God, he does not begin with a pedigree. He has no time for pedigrees. We nowhere find such words as "Jesus was born of so-and-so who was begat by so-and-so," because it had no meaning for the gospel of John. John begins with these words: In the beginning was the Word, and the Word was with God, and the Word was God. Then he goes on to say: And the Word became flesh and dwelt among us, and we beheld His glory, glory as of the only begotten of the Father—God the Son.

In Matthew the Holy Spirit uses it to interpret Jesus as the King, he does not take us too far back. He takes us to Abraham and we discover that Jesus has a whole pedigree that goes back to David and through David back to Abraham. That is all that is needed because He is a King, and a King has to have a pedigree. Now, of course, you do not know anything about kings on this side of the Atlantic, only that you had a Thanksgiving Day and got rid of him! On the other side we know quite a lot about kings. We would never accept someone to be crowned in Westminster Abbey in the United Kingdom if they did not have the right pedigree. A person cannot just appear from anywhere and say, "I am a member of the royal family." We want their pedigree; it is absolutely essential. So when Matthew reveals Jesus as King, as David's greater Son, as the One who will sit upon the throne of David forever, he gives us the pedigree and it is very important.

When Luke reveals Jesus by the Holy Spirit he is inspired to interpret Jesus as the Son of man. He gives a pedigree that goes right back, not only to David and Abraham, but beyond Abraham to Adam. This pedigree says, "He is man; He is not just and only Jewish, He is not just and only David's greater Son, and He is not only a Son of Abraham, He is a member as it were of the human race, going back to Adam.

But when Mark is inspired by the Holy Spirit to reveal Jesus as the Servant of the Lord, there is no pedigree whatsoever. Suddenly, at the beginning of Mark, dramatically and almost sensationally, we find Jesus is there. He goes out into the wilderness by the Spirit and meets Satan. It is almost as if it begins "just like that" with the words of John the Baptist making a highway for the Lord in the wilderness, preparing the way for the Messiah to come. Within a few verses of the opening chapter of Mark's gospel you will find Jesus and there is no pedigree. Why? Because God is saying, "I do not need a pedigree with a servant.

The thing that matters with a servant is not to know that he has blue blood, aristocratic, noble or royal blood; the thing that matters is that he has a hearing ear! If he cannot hear what I want him to do, what point is there in having a servant?" So we find from the very beginning that Jesus as the Servant of God is the One who hears the Lord. And because He hears the Lord, He is able to do the will of God. In that wonderful messianic Psalm we read these words: "Sacrifice and offering thou hast no delight in; Mine ears hast thou opened: Burnt-offering and sin-offering hast thou not required. Then said I, Lo, I am come; In the roll of the book it is written of me: I delight to do thy will, O my God; Yea, thy law is within my heart" (Psalm 40:6–8).

Service is Connected with Hearing

This little word "mine ears has thou opened" is very interesting in Hebrew. Because what it really says in a very awkward and strange way is: "my ears have you digged" or "my ears have you pierced through." You have done something to my ear. It is almost as if the Messiah was saying: "I delight to do thy will, O God, because you have done something to my ear." The ear has been opened.

I have already spoken about being a living sacrifice, but I want to add this. Do not get it wrong but hear what I am saying. You can be a living sacrifice, but if you do not hear the Lord, a lot of your being a living sacrifice is going to be ineffective. The Lord says sacrifice and offering thou hast no delight in. What the Lord delights in is exactly opposite to what we think. He says sacrifice and offering thou hast no delight in unless it leads to a pierced ear. Burnt offering and sin offering thou hast not required. Then said I, Lo, I am come to do thy will. I delight to do thy will, O my God; thy law is within my heart.

In Deuteronomy we have the picture of a servant who does not want to go out free. In the Jubilee year, the fiftieth year, all property and possessions return to their rightful owner and all slaves were free to go out. Now if they had a wife and children they had to remain with the master, but the actual slave was free to go out. However, if he loved his master he had to go to his master and say, "I will not go out free," and the master would take the servant to the gate post and pierce through his ear with an awl (Deuteronomy 15:16–17). In other words, he had a little ring pierced through his ear and this meant he was a voluntary slave or servant forever in the house of his master. Therefore, in the olden days when you saw a slave who had no ring in his ear, you knew he was just a purchased slave who was perhaps there under protest. But when you saw a slave with a gold ring through his ear, he was quite different. He was there because he wanted to be there.

Why did the Lord not put a ring through the nose? This was done in some parts of the world. A ring could be put through the nose or better still, round the neck. There could be a bangle around the arm, a ring on the finger, a ring on one of the toes, or a bangle round the ankle. Why through the ear? Because God was saying service is connected with hearing. So if he wants to be a servant forever then the master can say, "I have his ear." What point is it if you are called a servant of God and God does not have your ear? Do you have a pierced ear? It is vital that God get your ear! Long before He gets your foot and long before He gets your hand, He wants your ear.

Now we have this even more interestingly in Leviticus 14:14–17 with regard to the leper and the cleansing from leprosy. When the leper is delivered and healed from his leprosy, this is what has to take place: "And the priest shall take of the blood of the trespass-offering, and the priest shall put it upon the tip of the right ear of him that is to be cleansed, and upon the thumb of his right hand, and upon the great toe of his right foot" (v. 14).

Here we have ear, thumb, and toe. Will you notice the order? It is not toe, thumb, and ear, but ear, thumb and toe. If we can only get hold of this, it is so simple. God first wants your ear before He gets your hand and your foot. The trouble with us is that when we are leaders we want to be always doing something with our hands. "Let's get on with it. Come on, Lord! You know I do not want to sit here like Mary mystically listening. Let's get on with it! Put something in my hands, something I can do." Our feet have an itch in them. They want to run, they want to get on with things, get things done, and go places with God! God says, "It is no good. If you think you are going to go places with Me and work My works, the first thing I need is your ear." Therefore when He cleanses you from sin, the first thing that the blood touches is your hearing so that you can hear God. Then it touches your doing and your walking.

An Experience of the Holy Spirit

"And the priest shall take of the log of oil, and pour it into the palm of his own left hand; and the priest shall dip his right

finger in the oil that is in his left hand, and shall sprinkle of the
oil with his finger seven times before the Lord: and of the rest of
the oil that is in his hand shall the priest put upon the tip of the
right ear of him that is to be cleansed, and upon the thumb of
his right hand, and upon the great toe of his right foot, upon the
blood of the trespass-offering"
Leviticus 14:15–17

As we continue from verse 14 we find something more interesting. Will you notice that the Lord makes more of the oil than even of the blood? It is interesting that the blood is not poured into the palm and then sprinkled seven times before the Lord. But when it comes to the oil, the priest pours it into the palm of his left hand and he takes it with his right finger and sprinkles it seven times, meaning totality. He then takes the rest of the oil and puts it first on the ear, then on the thumb and then on the toe. All of this is done on the right side. Therefore you need not only be cleansed; you need an experience of the Holy Spirit. You need not only to know what the atonement, the saving grace of the Lord Jesus is for you, but you need to know the indwelling and empowering of the Holy Spirit. The Holy Spirit does not first set our feet dancing, itching to go places, or our hands itching to do things, but He first gets our ear! If the Holy Spirit does not have your ear, you are of no good whatsoever as far as the service of God is concerned. I am not saying you are not saved; I am just saying you are of absolutely no earthly or heavenly use to your Father. He could say, "I will follow Him"—but he cannot hear. I could shout at him "Do this!" But he cannot hear. He has got his hand so filled with the routine life of the church that he cannot even hear what I am saying. He has got his feet so filled with running here and there and doing this and that in the work of God he cannot hear what I am saying."

I must say that in the work of God wherever one goes, this is exactly what is found. People who began with such zeal, with such clarity, with such joy, with such longing and desire for God are now in a big routine. They have got to run here, they have got to run there, they have got to do this; they have got to do that. They are so busy they cannot hear God. They no longer hear Him— if they ever heard in the first place. This is because somehow their foot and their hand assumed priority, and God puts the priority on the ear.

Collective Leadership

Now suffer a word that I hope will not be too shocking. We believe in the plurality of leadership. We do not believe in the hierarchy system with one man and others under him. Now there is a first amongst equals which is obvious, and it is a spiritual matter. We make much of the equality of leadership, but amongst leaders there will always be those who have more experience and have a clearer way with God. They are not unfailingly right and that is why we need always to emphasize the equality of leadership; but generally speaking we give them respect.

Do you know what the great weakness of collective leadership is? Having now had thirty years of experience in watching, observing, and being part of it, the great weakness of collective leadership is in its being opportunist. It never has foresight. In other words, very rarely do you find collective leadership planning ahead. It always takes things as they come and uses them. For instance, I find again and again when I go different places that I am asked, "How come you can go so many days to so and so and you only have an hour for us?" And I reply, "Because they asked me two years ago!" I am using myself as an illustration, forgive me. We wait until we hear a brother is moving to another place and then we scramble, "Oh! Do you think you could come and give us a day or an hour or take this or that time?" We say, "How come he is going to so and so and doing this and that?" We are so busy with the routine life of the church and the responsibilities and burdens that we can never hear the Lord for anything ahead. It is a tremendous thing when brethren receive a burden for the future. I do not mean a far distant future, but they get a burden for something ahead. They feel, "It would be good if we had a sisters' weekend," or "it would be good if we had a young people's time," or "it would be good if we did this or that." In other words, they plan ahead for the needs of the flock.

The problem of collective leadership is that normally speaking there are three or four brothers, all inwardly in their heart a little afraid of taking the initiative lest the other brothers should think, "Ah! so and so is making a bid! Who does he think he is?" Hence we are always a little afraid, and of course we must all be broken, humble, and modest—which means we all sit in the back seat and nobody does anything. Therefore it is of tremendous importance for brethren to get to know each other, to get to understand each other, to be able to understand the temperament of each one and to be able to trust the Lord in one another. Then if a brother has a burden and says, "I think it would be so good if we were to do such and such," it could be taken up in prayer: "Is the Lord saying something?" This I believe is of tremendous importance.

So we have blood upon the right ear, upon the thumb of the right hand and on the great toe of the right foot. We have oil upon the right ear, upon the thumb of the right hand and upon the great toe of the right foot. In other words, God has cleansed our hearing that we may not be fashioned according to this world but be transformed by the renewing of our mind that we may prove what is the good and acceptable and perfect will of God (Romans 12:2).

Take a Step of Faith

If I may speak directly: I wish some of the brothers who have a problem hearing the Lord would take a step of faith and say, "I hear the Lord! I hear the Lord, and I am going to hear the Lord!"

There was a brother some years ago who was as deaf as a door post. Unless he saw you he never knew if you were coming up behind him. You could have hit him with a hammer from the back and he would not have known. He had three beautiful children and a lovely wife. I remember once he told me about his deafness. He said, "Do you know how I became deaf according to the specialist?" "No," I said. "Well, I was in a family of seventeen children and they were so noisy that at a very early age I just shut them all out." Within a matter of years he had become deaf.

I feel that there are many servants of the Lord who are like that. They say, "I cannot hear; I am not one of those special people like Stephen Kaung or Watchman Nee or others." We would not call them mystics in our circle, but perhaps we think of them as elite. They are the pioneers, they are the great ones, and they hear the Lord! "But I! I am a plebeian, you know, one of the great masses. I do not hear the Lord like that! I would drop dead if the Lord talked to me. He does not do it; I am just not that kind." Do you know what happens? You become deaf. The God-given capacity to hear the Lord is ignored and left in disuse so that in the end it ceases to function.

Take a step of faith and say, "I hear the Lord. God has given me this ability." Do not just ask Him for it, but say, "I have it by the grace of God, it is my birthright. I am standing into it. I am going to hear the Lord." Expect to hear the Lord. What a strange father it would be who never talked to his child. Yet some Christians believe they can go through the whole of life and He never says a word to them because they think they are too unworthy. They would say, "God in heaven does not speak to every child of His." But God in heaven says this: "My sheep hear my voice and I know them and they follow me."

Elijah

I will finally end with the most dramatic lesson in the whole Bible regarding this matter of hearing the Lord. It is of course the life of Elijah who sums up service. There are two men according to the Bible and according to Jewish tradition who sum up the whole service of God under the Old Covenant. One is Moses and the other is Elijah. This is not just legend, myth, or some Jewish fable. For when the Lord Jesus was transfigured in glory there was Moses representing all the patriarchs and lawmakers and Elijah representing all the prophets and communicators of the mind of God (Matthew 17:3). These two men who communed with Jesus on the Mount of Transfiguration were representing the whole service of God under the Old Covenant. Elijah is a supreme example of service, and when we look at him, what a marvelous picture he is. There is a little phrase that I find so wonderful in the life of Elijah. It appears a number of times but you will find one example in I Kings: "And Elijah the Tishbite, who was of the sojourners of Gilead, said unto Ahab, As the Lord, the God of Israel, liveth, before whom I stand, there shall not be dew nor rain these years, but according to my word" (17:1).

The God of Israel Before Whom I Stand

The little phrase that I love so much is "the Lord, the God of Israel, before whom I stand." Even when he was running he could say "before whom I stand." Even when he was doing great work it was "the Lord before whom I stand." In other words, his whole attitude was one of service: "I am in the presence of the Master. I stand in the presence of the Master. He has only to say one word and I will do it!" He did not say, "Now listen, Ahab! I stood before the Lord this morning in my quiet time." No, it was a consistent, ongoing continuous thing. He was aware of the Lord all the time. Now I do not mean every minute he was conscious of the Lord, but he knew he was standing in the presence of the Lord. If the Lord wanted to say something he could say it and Elijah would hear no matter what he was doing. He could have been up on the mountain or down in the valley. If we know anything about the kind of country that Elijah loved, we understand something of the type of man he was. He was a most remarkable man. For places to live He chose those that had the most dramatic and sensational history in the whole of Israel—Carmel, Cherith, and Sinai—wherever one goes it is so dramatic. This says something about the man—he was a rugged manly man.

Elijah was a man of action. I have often said I would love to meet Elijah and one day I shall. I think he must have been an incredible character if you know as I do all the country where he lived. He always chose the most dramatic country in the whole of the Promised Land in which to live. When you think that he outran Ahab's royal chariot—that was something! In the olden days horses were a mark of quality and aristocracy, and it was the great pride of the king to have Ahab stallions that could run like lightning. I think it is an amazing thing that that man, after the contest with the prophets of Baal on the Mount of Carmel and then that great prayer warfare, could then run something like seventeen miles and get to Jezreel before King Ahab did in his chariot. That is some man. (I know many are now taking up jogging but that was not jogging!) The man must have had a heart that was strong, a body like an ox, and he must have been in form like a cheetah. He must have been an incredible person. Think of this man who outran Ahab's royal chariot twenty miles after a tremendous confrontation which would have exhausted most of the servants of the Lord. Certainly I would have had to go to my bedroom and lay down for a few hours. But not Elijah! He ran like the wind (and he was not so young either), and he got to the royal palace before Ahab. When old Ahab came rolling in with all the horses sweating and frothing at the mouth—there was Elijah! Poor Ahab, no wonder he felt he was haunted by Elijah:

"I left you back there on Carmel, how come you are here?!" "I ran."
The Lord did not even transport and drop him like he did Philip
on one occasion. Elijah ran and he outran. That man was a man,
but he heard the Lord. So much for this idea that the manlier you
are the less you really hear the Lord. This man heard the Lord.
Let us look at a few instances:

"And the word of the Lord came unto him, saying,
Get thee hence, and turn thee eastward, and hide thyself
by the brook Cherith, that is before the Jordan"
I Kings 17:2–3

"And the word of the Lord came unto him, saying,
Arise, get thee to Zarephath, which belongeth to Sidon,
and dwell there: behold, I have commanded a widow
there to sustain thee"
I Kings 17:8–9

"And it came to pass after many days, that the
word of the Lord came to Elijah, in the third year, saying,
Go, show thyself unto Ahab"
I Kings 18:1a

This was a man who heard the Lord. It is no wonder he said "the
Lord before whom I stand," because he could hear the Lord. The
Lord would say, "Get down there, go there, and show yourself
to Ahab." Elijah was not continually saying, "I think I will give
Ahab another shock this morning. It's about time he had a few
spiritual fireworks just to let him know the God of Israel lives!

I will go and say to him, 'this, this and this.'" No, this was not at all the case. He had to do what God told him.

Elijah Prayed with Prayer

In the New Testament there is a very interesting little phrase found in James 5:17: "And Elijah, who was a man of like passion such as we, prayed in prayer that it might not rain for three years." What does it mean in the Greek "he prayed with prayer"? It is hard to understand. But even if we take the English phrase, he prayed with prayer, how can you pray with anything else? It is rather silly, is it not? If you are going to pray, you have to pray with prayer. So why does God put in a useless little word? It does not mean that literally: he prayed with prayer. In other words, he was praying in the prayer of the Holy Ghost. It was the will of God. He did not pray his own prayer; he could not just say, "No more rain! That will show them, this godless lot!" He could only say, "The heavens will not rain and there will be no dew," which, by the way, is very important because in Israel we do not have rain for eight months out of the year, but the dew keeps everything alive. Elijah said, "No rain and dew," which was disastrous. But he could only say that because it was the will of God. In the same way when he said, "Now let the rain come," it was the will of God that the three years be finished. In other words, here was a man who stood before the Lord and he was hearing the Lord.

Elijah's Confrontation Upon Mount Carmel

Most readers are familiar with the marvelous story of the confrontation upon Mount Carmel between Elijah and those powers of evil and darkness. You will remember how the fire of God fell out of heaven and consumed the burnt offering. When first the challenge came, Elijah said to them, "All right, you build an altar and I will build an altar; you call upon your gods and I will call upon the God of Israel." Then they built their altar and danced up and down and around it from sunrise to sunset. They cut themselves, they screamed, they shouted, they got into an ecstatic frenzy, and tried in every way possible to get the goddess of fertility and the gods in the heavens to somehow come down and burn up the sacrifice, but nothing happened. And Elijah was very irreverent and said some very naughty things. In the King James Version it is so correct but in the Hebrew it is really quite direct. He said, "Maybe he is gone on a tour," or, "Maybe he is deaf," and again, I am afraid he said, "Or maybe he is sitting on the toilet," which is what it says in Hebrew. The King James says, "Maybe he has turned aside." What kind of man was Elijah! My word! No wonder the prophets of Baal were furious with this man. How could they bring their gods into disrespect?! And Jezebel was sopping at the mouth—she had to put on new lipstick! (1 Kings 19:18-19).

Fire Fell From Heaven

Years ago when I was in Egypt we went to one of those moral leadership courses. We had the most liberal of all theologians and he told us, "Of course, we all know how the fire fell." I was terribly interested. Then he said, "We know that on Mt. Carmel there are benzene wells and the water that Elijah poured into the ditches was benzene; it was not water. You have never seen fire lick up water have you? But with benzene the fire licks it up." In other words, Elijah was a real old fraud. But the theologian never told us where the fire came from, so when it came to question time I asked, "Where did the fire come from?" He looked at me quite blankly and said, "Fire. Fire?" I said, "The fire that licked up the benzene." "Oh, hmm, I don't know—well I never thought about it." So I said, "Maybe it was Elijah's cigarette."

No, Elijah had a real confrontation with the powers of darkness and fire fell from heaven. It fell at the exact time of the evening sacrifice in the temple at Jerusalem, and at that moment it consumed everything! Then all the people said, "The Lord, the God of Israel, he is God." And Elijah said, "Take all the prophets and slay every one of them. Do not let one of them escape" (1 Kings 18:39–40). And they slew all eight hundred and fifty of the prophets of Baal.

Then a messenger fled down the motorway to the royal palace some twenty miles away and said to Jezebel, "Do you know what has happened?! All your favorite priests are dead!" So when Elijah arrived at the palace in front of Ahab, Jezebel sent him a little message. Do you know she did not even bother to go out and see him?

Jezebel

Now Jezebel was not a tank of a woman. Sometimes we get the idea that these ferocious women are like huge Russian athletes with muscles! You might think, "Any man would quake before one of them!" But not Jezebel. She was the flimsiest, most feminine woman; she floated on a cloud of perfume with painted nails, beautiful manicured hands, a beautiful face, and she was the tiniest most coquettish woman in society. You would not have thought that Elijah would be afraid. But she just sent a message by a servant and said, "So let the gods do to me, and more also, if I make not thy life as the life of one of them by tomorrow about this time" (I Kings 19:2). And Elijah!—this great man of God, this man who had been so used by God, this man who had seen so many signs and wonders, whose whole ministry was earthquake, wind and fire, ran for his life even faster than when he ran before the royal chariot! Out into the desert, right down to the south he ran as far as he possibly could until he flung himself under a juniper tree. He was so exhausted that God said to some of the angels, "Oh my word! Get down there quickly and cook supper for him!" Then the angel shook him and said, "Elijah, Elijah, we have cooked you breakfast." He ate it and it is amazing that he was not the least bit surprised about the angels, but he was frightened to death of Jezebel.

The Wrong Direction

God said to the angels, "Do not say a single negative thing. Do not say anything about him fleeing from Jezebel. He has gotten into such a state he cannot take it. He is so panic stricken we have got to help him go in the wrong direction." So they said, "Have a sleep, Elijah." He said, "I wish I could die. It is no good," and he fell asleep. Now of course this occurred during the daytime, because in the olden days no one would travel in that part of the world during the day. Thus he slept. Then the angels woke him and again said, "Elijah—another meal" (1 Kings 19:3–8). Not a word of rebuke. The Lord had helped him go in the wrong direction. It was as if the Lord said to the angels, "Nothing negative, I will get him at the other end." This is just like the time when the Lord got Peter when he should not have been fishing in Galilee (John 21:3–22). The Lord said, "Let him go. I will get him." It is also like the two going to Emmaus. They had no business going in the wrong direction, but the Lord got them (Acts 1:4; Luke 24:13–31). Sometimes we can go in the wrong direction and a true servant of the Lord will help us go that way because God will get us at the other end. I hope this will not be misunderstood.

Wind, Earthquake and Fire

Thus Elijah was going in the wrong direction for forty days and forty nights until he finally came to Mount Horeb where he recovered and had some of his calm restored. Then the Lord called to him: "Elijah!" "Yes, Lord?" "Who told you to come here? (The KJV says: "What doest thou here?") Did you hear me say, 'get thee to Horeb'?" Elijah with the shrewdness that belongs to the Jewish race never answered the question. He said, "Oh, Lord! Do you know what is happening in the land?! Everyone is dying left, right and center! They have killed all Your servants and cast down Your altars, and I...even I only am left!" Then the Lord said, "All right Elijah, stand where you are." And as he stood, there was a tremendous wind. Now the wind in Sinai can actually split rocks because it has such force. It came with such power that it hit the mountains and the rocks exploded, broke and rumbled down. Elijah loved every minute of it! "Oh Lord! This is terrific!" And the Lord said, "I was not in the wind; I caused it, but I was not in it." Then there came an earthquake and the whole place shook and heaved up and down. Mountains were going up and valleys were coming down; great crevices were opening and Elijah loved it. "Oh Lord!" he said, "this is terrific!" And the Lord said, "I caused it, but I am not in it." Then a fire roared up the mountain. You would have thought that Elijah would have fled into a cave and covered his head. Have you ever seen a forest fire? It roars like an express train with such power and velocity. But Elijah stood there erect and said, "Lord, this is tremendous! What a display of divine fireworks. It is terrific!" And the Lord said, "I caused it, Elijah, but I am not in it." And do you know that Elijah never bowed. It seems he quite enjoyed it like a firework display—tremendous! Then when the earthquake shook the whole place and still he did not bow. He just sort of said, "This is tremendous! Power! Power! Oh, the power!" Then there was a still, small voice. In Hebrew it is "a sound of gentle stillness." When Elijah heard the voice of God, he crumbled. He wrapped his mantle round his head, fell on his face before God and the Lord said, "Elijah, what are you doing here?" (See I Kings 19:9–14.)

In other words, remember what we said about anointing? He had no business being there. Who told him to come down there? Wind, fire, earthquake—Elijah was no stranger to that.

Would to God every servant of the Lord had a ministry like that—tornado-like force, the flame of fire and earthquake power in its effect. But God was saying, "Elijah, Elijah, you have missed the point of being a servant. You must hear." And Elijah said, "Oh Lord, I am the only one left. They have killed all the prophets and I am the last one." And God said to Elijah, "Elijah, there are seven thousand who have not bowed the knee to Baal." In other words, God was saying that there were seven thousand who could hear the voice of God (see 1 Kings 19:1–18).

This matter of seeing and hearing is all important! Most of us who are servants of the Lord long for tornado-like energy to come upon us and use us in our ministry, in our work, and in leadership. And we long for fire, as it were, to consume everything—a flame of fire that we may serve God acceptably, earthquake effects, as it were, in everything we touch. But seeing and hearing is far more important to God. Signs and wonders, whatever you like to call them are important; do not devalue them or despise them. But far more important in leadership in the servant of the Lord is a seeing heart and a hearing ear especially in the days we are moving into now. There are going to come those as angels of light and ministers of righteousness seeking to divide the flock of God, seeking to lead people astray. There will be all kinds of pressures upon people, there will be messianic movements and all kinds of weird things. There will be wonders and signs done, even by the powers of darkness, in the end. We need to be men and women who see the Lord and hear the Lord; for only in so doing can we lead the people of God aright.

Do we understand the message? The whole of that man's ministry was wind, gale force powers, and a tremendous earthquake ministry shaking whole nations, and turning society upside down by the word and works of God. Fire! It was the Holy Spirit in Person. But God was saying to Elijah, "You may have a ministry of wind, earthquake and fire, but if you do not hear My voice you are of no use to Me. Far more important is a voice that can be heard in your spirit than a mighty ministry like that. Then, Elijah, you would not have fled from Jezebel. If you had only heard Me, I would have told you to stand there."

We know Jezebel's end, that she was thrown out of the window by rebels and the dogs ate her (II Kings 9:30–37). It could have happened a few years earlier. Elijah could have stood there and God would have said, "I will tell you what to tell that Jezebel. Don't you worry! She is challenging Me, not you." But the man was so panic stricken he could not hear the Lord and he did the natural, spontaneous thing. He ran for his life and has presented us with one of the greatest lessons in the whole Bible regarding service: Having served God in the most tremendous way, we cannot hear Him.

The Secret was the Hearing

This matter of hearing the word of the Lord is all important. Not very much later the Lord said to Elijah with great humor, "Elijah, go and anoint Jehu to be king. Your Jezebel will be dead (it was Jehu who killed her), and anoint Elisha to take your place, and Elijah, just before you go, there is just one thing—there are seven thousand who have not bowed the knee to Baal" (I Kings 19:16–17). What God was really saying is this: "You said you were the only one left? There are seven thousand who hear Me." That was the secret.

It was the hearing. It is not even the seeing of great works and the mighty things that could devastate and somehow influence one. But in the end, as far as God was concerned, it was the people who heard Him who were the ones who could be kept pure. They were the ones who became the overcoming remnant. They were the ones who were the advanced party in the fulfillment of God's purpose. They heard the Lord and did His will.

There can be no matter more important than this matter of hearing the Lord, particularly in the days into which we are now moving. May God give us a hearing ear. May we be those who can hear what the Spirit is saying to the churches. I know we all hear people who say, "The Lord told me to do this, the Lord told me to do that," and the Lord has never told them any such thing. Therefore we have to remember that all that we hear needs to be submitted in fellowship. We need to learn to trust the Lord in one another so that we are preserved from delusion and deception and we are enabled together to do the will of God. He that doeth the will of God abideth forever.

5.
Love Your God

---

1 John 21:15–17

So when they had broken their fast, Jesus saith to Simon Peter, Simon, son of John, lovest thou me more than these? He saith unto him, Yea, Lord; thou knowest that I love thee.
He saith unto him, Feed my lambs. He saith to him again a second time, Simon, son of John, lovest thou me? He saith unto him, Yea, Lord; thou knowest that I love thee. He saith unto him, Tend my sheep. He saith unto him the third time, Simon, son of John, lovest thou me?

Peter was grieved because he said unto him the third time, Lovest thou me? And he said unto him, Lord, thou knowest all things; thou knowest that I love thee. Jesus saith unto him, Feed my sheep.

1 Corinthians 12:29–14

Are all apostles? are all prophets? are all teachers? are all workers of miracles? have all gifts of healings? do all speak with tongues? do all interpret? But desire eanestly the greater gifts.

And moreover a most excellent way show I unto you. If I speak with the tongues of men and of angels, but have not love, I am become sounding brass, or a clanging cymbal. And if I have the gift of prophecy, and know all mysteries and all knowledge; and if I have all faith, so as to remove mountains, but have not love, I am nothing. And if I bestow all my goods to feed the poor, and if I give my body to be burned, but have not love, it profiteth me nothing.

Love suffereth long, and is kind; love envieth not; love vaunteth not itself, is not puffed up, doth not behave itself unseemly, seeketh not its own, is not provoked, taketh not account of evil; rejoiceth not in unrighteousness, but rejoiceth with the truth; beareth all things, believeth all things, hopeth all things, endureth all things. Love never faileth: but whether there be prophecies, they shall be done away; whether there be tongues, they shall cease; whether there be knowledge, it shall be done away. For we know in part, and we prophesy in part; but when that which is perfect is come, that which is in part shall be done away.

When I was a child, I spake as a child, I felt as a child, I thought as a child: now that I am become a man, I have put away childish things. For now we see in a mirror, darkly; but then face to face: now I know in part; but then shall I know fully even as also I was fully known.

But now abideth faith, hope, love, these three; and the greatest of these is love. Follow after love.

Revelation 2:1–5
To the angel of the church in Ephesus write: These things saith he that holdeth the seven stars in his right hand, he that walketh

in the midst of the seven golden candlesticks: I know thy works, and thy toil and patience, and that thou canst not bear evil men, and didst try them that call themselves apostles, and they are not, and didst find them false; and thou hast patience and didst bear for my name's sake, and hast not grown weary. But I have this against thee, that thou didst leave thy first love. Remember therefore whence thou art fallen, and repent and do the first works; or else I come to thee, and will move thy [lampstand] out of its place, except thou repent.

Shall we bow together in a word of prayer:

Heavenly Father, we do need You. We have already expressed our dependence upon You in our worship and praise and in the prayer that we have made to You. But Lord, when we come to Your Word we do want to confess once again we need Your presence because in many ways we have all heard this truth many times. It needs Your Holy Spirit to speak it into our hearts and challenge us in the deepest part of our being. And oh Lord, we pray together that You will deliver this time from anything in the atmosphere or anything in our situation or condition that could frustrate Your purpose. We commit ourselves to You, oh Lord, and take once more by faith, that anointing grace and power for both speaking and hearing. Fulfill Your purpose in this time, Lord. Draw near to every one of us, and Lord, may we remember these few days together here in this place. May it leave an indelible impression and mark upon our lives and upon our service.

Oh Lord, hear us. We ask it together in that glorious and marvelous name of our Lord Jesus. Amen.

I have spoken in these times concerning essential and fundamental characteristics of service. We have only had three sessions and therefore we have had to confine ourselves to three essential characteristics, but I wonder whether that may not be good. Very often when we have more time available and we can speak about some other characteristics, we can lose really what is priority. And therefore because we have not had so much time we have confined ourselves to three essential characteristics at least as the Lord has spoken in my heart and revealed something of the nature of this matter to me.

A Living Sacrifice

The first characteristic was the question of being a living sacrifice. We cannot get around it, we cannot bypass it, it is impossible to ignore this matter if we are going to serve the Lord. All real service flows out of being a living sacrifice. Otherwise we can start with the highest ideals and the greatest zeal and the greatest devotion, but because we have mixed motives and because we never become aware of some of the determining factors and influences in our services, those very things become the weakness upon which the enemy works in the end to undo us and to destroy our service. The only key to real service is to be a living sacrifice. No one can follow the Lord very far before he discovers the cross in his path. And either you will turn back or you will go out of the way or you will go on with the Lord. And in this matter we have spoken quite a bit about a living sacrifice.

A Hearing Ear

Then I spoke about another essential characteristic which is a hearing ear. We need a hearing ear to hear the Lord. There are very, very few Christians who hear the Lord. And yet Jesus said, "My sheep hear my voice and I know them and they follow Me." Every one of us has the spiritual apparatus, the spiritual capacity, the spiritual ability within our spirit to hear the Lord. It is very, very important that we should be able to hear what He is saying. How interesting it is that each of those messages to the seven churches ends with the refrain, he that hath an ear to hear, let him hear what the Spirit says to the churches (Revelation 2–3). It is so important to hear what the Lord is saying.

Elijah learned this tremendous lesson. His was a tremendous ministry lived in the presence of the Lord. He was always speaking about the Lord before whom I stand, and the Lord was always telling him, go here and then go there or show yourself to so-and-so or do this. Elijah is the symbol of service in the Old Testament along with Moses. He and Moses were the summing up of all true and genuine service under the Old Covenant and indeed in many senses in the whole Bible. But Elijah's greatest lesson was at the end of his ministry when after that terrific confrontation with the powers of darkness on Mt. Carmel in which God consumed the offering with fire from heaven and the priests of Baal were destroyed, one word from a very feminine lady, Jezebel, and the great servant of God fled for his life. God caught him at the end going as far as he could in the wrong direction. There was the great wind the Lord had produced that split the rocks, but the Lord was not in the wind. And there was a great earthquake which just simply shook everything and turned everything upside down. The Lord produced the earthquake, but the Lord was not in the earthquake. And then there was a great fire which roared up the mountainside which the Lord had produced, but the Lord was not in the fire. And Elijah remained erect through all of this. He enjoyed every moment of it; after all his whole ministry was wind, earthquake and fire. He was used to that powerful gale-like force. Ahab thought of Elijah as a gale-like force sweeping in, as it were, splitting everything, tearing everything down, and flattening everything. He thought of him as an earthquake turning the whole stable society in his eyes upside down. He thought of him as fire. But it was only when God spoke to Elijah in a still small voice that Elijah was broken, and then the lesson came home to him. In that moment of panic when Jezebel confronted him, he had not listened to the Lord. He had just done the natural spontaneous thing—panic. It is a tremendous lesson to learn.

You can have a ministry, which I imagine every single one who is a leader, everyone who is a servant of the Lord would love to have a ministry exemplified by gale-force wind, by earthquake-power and by fire. But that is not what God wants. God will use all that but what He wants is a hearing ear. The rest does not mean too much if there is not a hearing ear.

The Matter of Love

A third essential and fundamental characteristic of service is one that I fear almost to talk about because it is so simple. In fact all these ones we have talked about have all been so simple, so kindergarten, so Sunday school, and that is why I felt the need to pray before every time that the Lord would bring it home to us. It is so easy to say, "Oh, we have heard all this," and shut it out. But the fact of the matter is that these very simple truths are the vital ones. In the guise of going on with the Lord into the depths, we can ignore in reality these very simple truths that are absolutely essential.

And this matter of love is absolutely essential. It is very interesting in Mark's Gospel, chapter 12, almost the last words that Jesus ever spoke before He preached that tremendous message of denunciation is on this matter of love. The last positive words He ever spoke closing as it were His spoken public ministry, His Messianic ministry, were in answer to a good scribe who came to him and said: "And one of the scribes came, and heard them questioning together, and knowing that he had answered them well, asked him, What commandment is the first of all? Jesus answered, The first is, Hear, O Israel; The Lord our God, the Lord is one: and thou shalt love the Lord thy God with all thy heart, and with all thy soul, and with all thy mind, and with all thy strength. The second is this, Thou shalt love thy neighbor as thyself. There is none other commandment greater than these" (vv. 28–31).

Now for those of us who are Jewish it is very interesting because Mark is the only synoptic gospel which gives the full account of the answer of Jesus. For when Jesus was asked what is the greatest commandment He simply answered by reciting the creed. It is called in Jewish circles the Shemah: Hear, O Israel: the Lord thy God, the Lord, is one. Thou shalt love the Lord thy God with all thy heart, and with all thy soul, and with all thy mind and with all thy strength (see Deuteronomy 6:4–5). And then He added this other: And the second is like to it, thou shalt love thy neighbor as thyself.

Matthew adds an interesting little point: "Jesus said, Upon these two hang the whole law and prophets" (Matthew 22:40), as though the Lord Jesus was closing His ministry and going back to the roots. Thou shalt love the Lord thy God with all thy heart, with all thy soul, with all thy mind and with all thy strength, and thou shalt love thy neighbor as thyself.

The Answer to Burnout and Drudgery

I wonder whether for most of us it has sunk in. This whole question of burnout that we have been talking about really has no answer. We can divest ourselves of uncommanded works, we can delegate responsibility, but in the end we can still be burnouts. There is no real answer to the drudgery of service unless we love the Lord. It is as simple as that. If any of you expect to have a different experience to all the rest of us, you are going to be disillusioned. Most people who are not in leadership or do not have responsibility of one kind or another in the work long to have such responsibility or such position, but once you have got there you are not there very long before you suddenly discover that it is quite irksome; it is a drudgery and it has a routine.

It is a matter of responsibilities to be discharged and duties to be fulfilled.

There is in fact only one answer to the whole thing and that is to love the Lord your God with all your heart, with all your soul, with all your mind and with all your strength, and to love your neighbor as yourself. I see no other answer. This is the only way that all the drudgery of the routine is gilded. It is rather like a person who is running a home. One person finds it a drudgery and another person finds it fulfillment. What is the difference? One person loves her husband and her children and the other has fallen out of love with her husband and children. It is as simple as that. And the thing has just become a drudgery. There are the same chores, the same duties, the same responsibilities, but one person is in love and one person is out of love. The person in love has all the routine things to do like the other person but somehow or other finds fulfillment and joy in it because the dynamic of the whole thing is love. It is love that draws a person to be a sacrifice and love that draws a person to hear what is really said. There is no way of getting round this matter of love. It is strategically important.

John's Interpretation of Love

John's gospel is not a synoptic gospel. In other words, it is not a history but an interpretation. When John wrote his gospel, from the very beginning he wrote it not as a history, nor in chronological order, but as an interpretation. He takes the eight claims of Jesus: I am the bread of life, I am the light of the world, I am the door, I am the good shepherd, I am the resurrection and the life, I am the way, the truth and the life, before Abraham was I am, I am the vine. And then around them he groups signs. He does not call them miracles as in the other gospels or even wonders, he calls them signs because they signify something; they reveal the nature of the Lord Jesus and the tremendous work of the Messiah. And when he comes to the end of his gospel, he ends it in a most remarkable way. Instead of giving us the great commission that the others do such as Matthew gives us in chapter 28: "All authority and power is given unto me in heaven and on earth. Go ye therefore, and make disciples of all the nations, baptizing them into the name of the father and of the Son and of the Holy Spirit: teaching them to observe all things whatsoever I commanded you: and lo, I am with you always, even unto the end of the world" (vv. 18–20).

John does not end like that. Instead he tells us a story which is a real story; it is not a parable. The story is all to do with Peter and that is how he ends his gospel. Peter had done, as always, what he had been told not to do. Jesus had told them that they were to remain in Jerusalem. And Peter did remain in Jerusalem for a while, but he got fed up with it and said to the others, "I am going fishing." And the others said, "We will go with you." And so he went in the wrong direction just as Elijah went in the wrong direction only to find the Lord was at the other end. There was no rebuke. In fact, the wonderful thing about the Lord was that He cooked their breakfast just like the angels cooked Elijah's breakfast as he was going in the wrong direction, and as the Lord broke the bread with the disciples in Emmaus who were also going in the wrong direction. Is not the Lord wonderful! When we go in the wrong direction it is not like so many Christians who beat you black and blue, tell you why you are wrong and how you should be doing this and where you should be going. The Lord sometimes cooks us a meal and helps us in the wrong direction because He knows He is going to get us in the end.

The Lord Digs Deep in Peter on this Matter of Love

And here He cooks them a breakfast and they come to Him and eat. It is just like the Lord to give you a good meal first before He comes to the point. Then He says, "Simon, son of John, do you love me more than all these?" Now He could have meant more than all these other disciples or He could have meant more than all these other things, but it is just left: "Do you love me more than all?" Jesus used the word for a complete full love which you do not get in your English version. And when Peter answered, he said, "Lord, you know I have an affection for you." The Lord ignored it and said, "Feed my lambs." And then He said again, "Simon, son of John, do you love me?" And Peter said, "Lord, you know I have an affection for you." And Jesus said to him, "Tend my sheep." And then Jesus said it for the third time, only this time with a difference. It is just like our Lord; He came down to Peter's level: "Simon, son of John, do you have an affection for me?" And that irritated Peter. "Lord!" he said, "You know everything! You know I have an affection for you." "Feed my sheep." And that is how the gospel ends—this most magnificent of the gospels. This gospel that takes us to the very heart of God is how it ends. It is almost an anticlimax I imagine in some people's eyes. Why in the world don't we see Jesus in all His glory and power absolutely filling the universe as God the Son! But no, that is not how John's gospel ends. This tremendous revelation of the Person of the Lord Jesus, this tremendous interpretation of Jesus as God Himself, manifest in the flesh, ends with this amazing incident: "Simon, son of John, do you love me more than all?" "Lord, you know I have an affection for you." "Tend my lambs." In other words, it was the commission that we have in Matthew, Mark and in Luke, only this again is an interpretation. It is as if the Lord Jesus was saying "I do not want you going to the ends of the earth and giving your body to be burned as a martyr or bestowing all your goods to feed the poor, or knowing all knowledge and all mysteries; I want your heart! If it is not out of love for Me—first love—it means nothing."

The Key for All True Service

How easily the Lord could have said to Simon, "Simon, son of John, do you love this flock more than anything else?" And then He could have said, "Well, feed them." But Jesus did not say that. It is not love for the flock that is to be the basis of our service; it is love for Him. If you only have love for the flock, I will guarantee one thing, you will fall out of love very rapidly. Sheep are sheep, and you will not stay in love with them for very long. And the Lord knew that. There is only one way that we shall ever fulfill the ministry that is given to us: run the race and finish the course (that is if we remain in the love of God). There is no other way. That is the key to all service. And I hope that although this is kindergarten in many ways, it will burn into your hearts and you will never forget it. You may hear a million other messages, but

I hope you will never forget this simple little message that the heart and the key of all true service is love for God. If you do not remain in love with the Lord Jesus, it will become drudgery and you will spend your whole time trying to get out of it. You will think of every exit possible, every excuse possible, how to backtrack, how to get out of the predicament you have gotten into by jumping too quickly into serving the Lord.

Sheep and Lambs

Sheep and lambs are the whole flock. It is interesting how the Lord put it. Lambs and sheep cover the whole flock: babies and adults. The Lord never said anything about the condition of them, I take it some were nice tempered and some were bad tempered. Some were difficult and some were not so difficult, but they are all in the flock. He divided them only by lambs and sheep.

Feed and Tend

Then there are these two words: feed and tend. Now it is easier to feed the flock than tend it. Feeding the flock is not too hard of a job. In the part of the world that I come from you can often see the shepherds leading out their flocks to the mountainside and into the wadi. It is a reasonably pleasant occupation, but it requires a bit of foresight. The flocks south of me, which is the Bethlehem area, move up to the north of Jerusalem to Ramallah, and twice a year they go through the very area where I live which is an awful nuisance as far as we are concerned because the sheep and the goats leave a whole lot of chips which the dog picks up when she goes out. And so we are always annoyed every spring and every fall when the flocks go through. Of course, why they do it now that the area is built up I do not know, but they have been doing it for thousands of years and they do not feel like changing the track. So now it happens to be a national park, but it does not stop the shepherds who for thousands of years have driven their flocks right through the park. They go up through the Ramallah area for the summer and they are in the Bethlehem area for the winter. Finding food for the flock is a reasonably pleasant occupation. It is the tending of the sheep that is the difficult thing. One of the things I have learned from some of the shepherds is that sheep have to be inspected regularly. You cannot go more than forty-eight hours without inspecting them. They develop foot rot almost overnight, so they have to be inspected almost daily.

Now goats are interesting. You can leave them almost two weeks because they are basically disease free. But sheep have to be inspected the whole time. That is what the Lord meant when He said "tend." There are a whole lot of things involved in this tending and feeding of lambs and sheep. There is health and well-being, there is protection and security, there is correction and there is food, and the food side requires a bit of foresight. The shepherd has to know where the grass and pasture is good and where it is not too sparse that year. He has to think where there is plenty of water, at least enough, to water the flocks. He has to know where there are wells and how long the wells were not dry. Springs are a very localized business. In some places they will last for a month or two, in other places they will last longer. Some years wells will dry up more quickly than others. So it is not just a question of going on a little track; he has got to have a little bit of foresight, a little bit of thought. The shepherd's job is not just some empty-headed job.

Lambs and sheep, feeding and tending. And the amazing thing is who would have ever related love to that job? "Lovest thou me more than all these? Feed my lambs, tend my sheep, feed my sheep." When you come to the marvelous letter to the Corinthians, in chapter eleven the apostle starts to take up the whole question of the church, the body of the Lord Jesus, its function, its gifts, the various contributions that have to be made for its well-being. He goes through it all, but how interesting it is that right in the middle of it all we have this amazing poem on love.

A Poem on Love

Now, if we did not know the Lord, we could be forgiven for wondering if somehow or other this got misplaced. What in the world is this doing here in the middle of all this talk about the body of Christ, about all the members of the body being many are only one body in Christ and about the hand not being able to say to the eye I have no need of you, or the ear being able to say to the foot, I have no need of you? What has this all got to do with this amazing matter of love? But right in the heart of it all the apostle says, "Desire earnestly the greater gifts, but a more excellent way I will show you." And he ends it with these words as it is in Phillips translation: "Make love your aim. If I speak with the tongues of men and of angels, but have not love, I am become sounding brass, or a clanging cymbal." In other words, I can speak in tongues but if there is no love, then it is just empty. Or listen to this: "And if I have the gift of prophecy, and know all mysteries and all knowledge; and if I have all faith, so as to remove mountains, but have not love, I am nothing." I imagine most servants of the Lord would give anything to have the gift of prophecy and know all mysteries and all knowledge. What a fund for servants. What a marvelous storeroom to draw from when you preach, to know all mysteries and all knowledge and have the gift of prophecy, and imagine having all faith so as to remove mountains. There are many spiritual obstacles confronting assemblies and fellowships represented in this little time together. Can you imagine what it would mean if we had all faith so as to remove those obstacles? But listen to what the word says: "If I have the gift of prophecy and know all mysteries—the mystery of Christ, the mystery of the church, the mystery of Israel—and all knowledge; and if I have all faith, so as to remove mountains, but have not love, I am nothing."

Useless Without Love

Let it sink in. Nothing! That means I can have such a knowledge of mysteries that I could dazzle you with my understanding of the things of God and the depths of God! I could have such faith that I could do signs and wonders one after the other that would cause you to stand in awe, but if it is not done out of love for Him, then God says it is worth nothing. I imagine that most of us subconsciously think that if we could do all these things at least we will get some commendation when we finally get there. And the Lord would say, "Well, you were rather poor on this and this, but I must say you did have the gift of prophecy and you did use it; you did have an understanding of those mysteries and of knowledge and you did use it; you did have faith and removed mountains; I think these are commendable!" But if I understand the Word of God, it says this: The Lord will say, "You had all that faith and you removed mountains, you had all that knowledge of mysteries and of these other things, you had the gift of prophecy, you had the gift of tongues, but you did not have love, and it means absolutely nothing! You might as well not have done it! It is worthless!" Then my dear friends, the drudgery of our routine service is nonsensical. We might as well get out of it right now and start to enjoy ourselves.

God's Love is an Awesome Thing

The trouble is, if we are believers we cannot get out of it. This is the problem. Most preachers would never say this, but it is the problem, is it not? The fact is that we have an enemy; we are marked people. We can try to say, "I think I will just get out of this; it is ridiculous. I do not feel I really love the Lord as I ought to, and the whole thing has become a drudgery. I am going to get out and enjoy myself." I will tell you one thing. You may be out tonight, and for the next six months you will have a whale of a time and then the enemy will get you. Step by step, stage by stage, he will destroy you. This is the problem of being a believer. Once God has called you there is no escape; you might as well go on. It is an amazing thing. I always say to people that it is both at one and the same time the most wonderful thing in the world to be loved by God and the most horrific. It is so wonderful that God loves me; but it is an awesome thing that He loves me because He will not be frustrated. He will wait and even if it is on my deathbed He is going to get me. So He might as well get me now. If He is going to love like that, what is the point of holding out until my deathbed? It is better to give in right now and say, "Lord, I will go with You the whole way."

The whole problem is very simply this: What is the point for this drudgery of all these duties and responsibilities and this possibility of burnout? If we get out of it we shall be happy for a little while only to find ourselves destroyed at the end by the one who hates the Lord Jesus and hates the very mark of the Lord Jesus in us even when we have fallen away. So full of hatred is the enemy for anyone who is marked with the name of the Lord Jesus that even when that one gives himself over as it were to the other side, Satan will still destroy him. We are caught. Now this is our predicament as servants of the Lord.

I can have the gift of prophecy and know all mysteries and all knowledge and I can have all faith so as to remove mountains but if I have not love I am nothing. What are we going to do? And if I bestow all my goods to feed the poor—now you would have thought that would have got a commendation from the Lord. Think of it. If we just suddenly go home and say, "I will sell the lot and give it to the poor." And if I give my body to be burned— can you believe it? Do you realize what the inspired Word is saying? If I give my body to be burned—most of us would say, "Oh! How amazing! He was a martyr." And the Lord says, "It is worthless. Worthless!" Do you know there are some people who are so given to an ideal that they could become martyrs? But it is not out of love for the Lord. There are the kind that grit their teeth and sort of say once they are challenged, "I am going through this no matter what happens." And the more you challenge them, the more they are determined to go through it. They are not going to give up! But it has nothing to do with loving the Lord. Someone has challenged them on this thing! It is that type of thing. There are plenty of Iranian martyrs. All through history there have been people who have given their bodies to be burned and others who have bestowed all their goods. It is not that it is wrong, but I want you to get the message. "And if I bestow all my goods to the feed the poor, and if I give my body to be burned but have not love, it profits me nothing."

Love Never Fails

"Love suffereth long, and is kind; love envieth not; love vaunteth not itself, is not puffed up, doth not behave itself unseemly, seeketh not its own, is not provoked, taketh not account of evil; rejoiceth not in unrighteousness, but rejoiceth with the truth; beareth all things, believeth all things, hopeth all things, endureth all things. Love never faileth" (1 Corinthians 13 4–8).

Now we talk about burnout, about the weariness of leadership responsibilities, about the drudgery of service, but this kind of love is the only thing that transforms it and makes it a privilege to serve the Lord. It is not a question of you thinking of your goods that you are bestowing on the poor or your body that will be burned or the exercise of prophecy; it is a spontaneous exercise of love. Love never fails. And take note of where this amazing revelation comes. It is placed right in the midst of one of the supreme passages on the functioning of the body of the Lord Jesus on this earth. This love preserves us from getting so tangled, so sound and correct and right and perfect in performance. The key is love. Desire earnestly the greater gifts but a most excellent way show I unto you. Make love your aim. Yet desire earnestly spiritual gifts. I have to bring myself back to this thing, as I think you have to come face to face with it, again and again. There is no other way through.

Ephesus Lost Their First Love

Consider this whole question of the Lord's message to the first church in Revelation 2 to which the Lord Jesus says all these marvelous things: "I know thy works and thy toil and endurance." Now I think that is pretty good because I know many churches who have none of these things. "I know thy works, and thy toil and endurance, and that thou canst not bear evil men, and didst try them that call themselves apostles, and they are not, and didst find them false; and thou hast endurance and didst bear for my name's sake, and hast not grown weary."

Now that is not a burnout. They have not yet got there. They have not yet even grown weary. But the interesting thing is this, the Lord says, "I have this against you, that you left your first love. Remember therefore whence thou art fallen, and repent and do the first works; or else I come to thee, and will move thy lampstand out of its place" (vv. 2–5).

This church has so much to commend it. Works, toil, endurance, it has not grown weary, it sorted out the precious from the vile, it has rejected the false and the erroneous and held to the true and the genuine. Nevertheless, the Lord says, "I have this against you; you have fallen from your first love. Repent and do the first works or else I will come and remove your lampstand out of its place."

First Love

Now I wonder whether many of us feel that this is unnecessarily harsh to rebuke them and warn them that the lampstand could be removed out of its place simply because they have left their first love. Now first love is not a question of time. In other words, you have first love and then you have another kind of love, and then you have finished or maturing love. First love is a quality of love. When people have first love, when they really fall in love, there are all kinds of things that happen. They do the most ridiculous things they would never have dreamed of doing. For instance, some men would not go near a shop, not in a thousand years, but when they fall in love, lo and behold they are trailing around shops with their beloved. It is true, it will only be for a month of two, but nevertheless in that first love they are doing things they would never dream of doing normally. When people are in first love, they do not even think about eating; their appetite seems to have completely disappeared. It is amazing, but it is first love. It does not necessarily continue, thank God, or they would die! But that is the effect first love has on them. There are a thousand and one things that happen when people are in love. It is first love. When people have first love, nothing is too great a trouble. A person will travel forty-fifty miles to meet their beloved or they will travel half the globe to do something for them. Nothing is too much trouble. Nothing is a drudgery. Nothing is a duty. Nothing is a responsibility. Who talks about responsibilities or duties when you are in love? There is no such thing. And as for drudgery, you would never think of such a thing. Drudgery?! You would never think of such a thing. It is first love. It is only when the first love has gone that we start to talk about duties, responsibilities, chores, the routine, the difficulties, the problems or the obstacles. The catalogue is endless once we have got out of first love. And we are all caught. We have spent this whole weekend talking about duties and responsibilities and chores and the drudgery of the routine of service and the possibilities of burnout and all the other things. It is endless. We have to confess it. Something has happened to our first love.

The Marriage and the Bride

It is interesting that when the Bible ends, it ends with a marriage and a bride. But before the Lord speaks of the city, He speaks of the bride. It is almost as if the Lord is saying, "I want people to come to the place where they can rule with Me, where they can reign with Me, where they can govern with Me, where they can know My heart and My mind and administer My will according to My heart and mind. I do not want people who can do all this out of their knowledge; I want people who are in love with Me." The bride is there because she chose to be there. However it is an amazing paradox. She is really there because the Lord chose her, but she is also there because she chose to be there. Having been chosen by Him, she then says, "I choose to be with You, and I will follow You withersoever You go, placing my steps in your steps. Where You go I will go, where You lie down, I will lie down; Your people will be my people."

It is extraordinary to me that the Bible ends on this note so that the whole of eternity opens up with all its glorious possibilities and potentialities. And we are not told anything about what they will do except that the Lamb goes out with His wife into that eternity. It is going to be marvelous, and I believe it is going to be marvelous because the Lord has gone to such extraordinary lengths to get His bride. He endured six thousand years at least of misery, of disorder, of sin, of wickedness, of iniquity, and then sent His only Son into the world to die on the cross to obtain such a people for Himself. I cannot believe then that all we are going to do is play harps forever and ever and ever and sing eternal hallelujah choruses. Some of these hymns that we are speaking of—walking up and down the golden streets and tramping in and out of the pearly gates—are hard to sing. Now I know that music is very satisfying and very beautiful, but endless singing? I cannot believe that the Lord has gone to all this trouble just for that.

The Bride that God Wants for His Son

He says, "I make all things new." Now if this world in its fallen state is so marvelous, so wonderful, so incredibly beautiful, what is it going to be like when it all becomes new? The thought of it blows your mind. And at the heart of this new heaven and new earth is a city, a bride. It is not someone who has been redeemed but is totally empty-headed, some pretty little doll that can sit next to the King of the Universe and look sweet like some kind of puppet, as if the Lord would be interested in such a bride! He could have taken Adam and Eve and created such a puppet right at the start if He had really wanted such an empty-headed little Hollywood doll to sit beside Him, looking all beautiful with people saying, "Isn't she lovely?!" But the poor thing cannot say two words; all she can do is smile sweetly. She is just a proper little empty-headed doll, and that is all. However, that is the idea one gets from certain Christian writings. That is all the church is meant to be; reduced of all originality, devalued of every single thing that could be said to be hers, making her a channel only. He is going to do everything while she just sits there draping the throne as a trophy of grace. Some trophy! No wonder the agnostics and atheists hold the whole gospel up to ridicule when they hear that kind of thing as if that is the gospel. It is nonsensical. If He had wanted that kind of empty-headed dumbbell, He could have created that kind of creature at the very beginning. But instead, He has endured at least six thousand years of human history with all its ups and downs, all its wickedness, He sent the Lord Jesus into the world who gave Himself for our sin and when He died, they pierced His side out of which came blood and water. And John says there are three that bear witness, the spirit, the water and the blood (1 John 5:8). That is the bride who is being created by the Spirit out of the water and blood that flowed from the side of Jesus.

I believe that at the heart of this new heaven and new earth there will be millions and millions of saved ones who have never grown up. They will enjoy it and God will enjoy them, but at the heart of that whole family there will be a bride. She is made up of those who have walked with the Lamb the whole way. She chose to be there because He chose her. She said, "I want to be there with You just because it is You. I want to be there, and I want to serve You. I am never going to talk about drudgery or duties or responsibilities or chores, even though I may be filled with the whole thing. I want to be so in love with You that it will be a privilege to do all these things from the humblest to the most difficult and great things. I want to be with You."

Union and Communion

I cannot believe that anything less than that would satisfy the heart of the Lord. He wants a union and communion (if you understand what I mean) between equals. I do not want to take away from the glory of the Lord Jesus, but what I want to get over to you is that God wants to produce a bride that is made up out of His own nature, out of His own life, with His own character, able to commune with Him, able to understand Him, able somehow to sense His will and able to administer it with Him. I do not know what we shall do in eternity of eternity. I know some of the prophets talk about strange things. They talk about trees clapping their hands and hills singing for joy, and some people think that is only poetry, but I wonder if there is a bit more in it than that. For the apostle Paul says the whole of the natural creation groaneth in travail together until now waiting for its place of adoption, its recognition, the recognition of the sons. What on earth does it mean? Does it mean that somehow one day when this whole natural creation is no longer subjected to the cycle of futility and corruption it will evolve into something else? I do not know. Sufficient for me is that it will be wonderful to be with the Lord to see it all and be involved in the production of it all, to be involved, if you like, in a right way in the evolution of it all and to see the whole thing from the heart.

Service therefore is a preparation. Leadership is a preparation. It does not mean that because you are a leader here you will be a leader there although generally speaking if the Lord really is going to train you in those qualities He wants you to be one there. And so this whole matter finally comes down to this: "Do you love me? Do you love me more than all? Feed my lambs. Do you love me? Tend my sheep. Do you love me? Feed my sheep."

We cannot get away from it. "Hear, O Israel: the Lord thy God, the Lord, is one. Thou shalt love the Lord thy God with all thy heart, with all thy soul, with all thy mind, with all thy strength and thou shalt love thy neighbor as thyself" (Mark 12:29–31).

6.
The Role of Elders

Take heed unto yourselves, and to all the flock, in which the
Holy Spirit hath made you bishops [or overseers], to feed the
church of the Lord which he purchased with his own blood.
I know that after my departing grievous wolves shall enter
in among you, not sparing the flock; and from among
your own selves shall men arise, speaking perverse things,
to draw away the disciples after them...Wherefore watch ye.
Acts 20:28–31a

Exhortation to the Elders at the Church of Ephesus

This is the church at Ephesus which was one of the churches that had perhaps the deepest and fullest spiritual character of all the churches in the New Testament. Here we have the words spoken by the Holy Spirit through the apostle Paul to the elders. You will notice in Acts 20:17–18 that he called to him the elders of the church and when they were come to him, in the course of other things he said in verse 28: "Take heed unto yourselves, and to all the flock, in which the Holy Spirit hath made you bishops [or overseers]" which is the meaning of the word bishop, that is, someone who watches over the whole—to feed the church of the Lord which he purchased with his own blood. He then says a very interesting thing: "I know that after I have gone grievous wolves shall enter in among you, not sparing the flock." Now this company was well taught enough not to be easily taken in, and yet there were those who were going to come in who really did not care for the flock but actually wanted to devour them. They were not there to feed the flock; they were there to feed on the flock and that is a great difference. And in Christian work there are brethren whom I fear are amongst the people of God to feed on them and from them, to devour them, instead of feeding the flock which is our calling.

Another very interesting thing about this is that he also says, "From among your own selves shall men arise, speaking perverse things." Which this is an indication of the freedom of their gatherings, showing that they were so free there could rise amongst them people who could say false things.

Fear Comes into the Church When There is Change

Now this is a good word because we have been meeting together at Halford House for over twenty-five years. We have had a real history with the Lord, but I think some of you older ones, especially those of you who have been with us from the beginning and had that original experience and all that God did, have a little fear in your hearts because I have been taken away more. You may be saying, "Oh, dear, dear, are we going to be safe? Are we going to be secure? Maybe this will happen, maybe that will happen, maybe the other will happen." I am sure the church at Ephesus (not that I am speaking of myself as being in the category of the apostle Paul), might have felt far more secure if the apostle Paul would have stayed. If he had been around he could have dealt with any problem or difficulty. Those who were with the apostle right at the beginning when the church was born must have had a relationship with him. Furthermore, I am quite sure you understand the spiritual character of these people. That such a letter like the Ephesian letter could be written to them indicates a spiritual character and capacity on their part. Surely you are not going to tell me that when the apostle Paul left them they did not feel, "Oh, dear, now what is going to happen?" And this is one of our problems. Because we do not trust the Lord, those of us who are older in the Lord and have been here right from the beginning, actually paralyze the way of the Lord ahead. It is the easiest thing to define the faults, weaknesses and failings of the brethren and feel they are losing this or that and start to feel, "Oh, dear;" then fear spreads to us all. Then there are some people who want to move into an altogether new way and leave everything, and other people who want to hold on to the old format.

The Key is to Trust the Lord

We need to be together, but it is more than being together; the key is to trust the Lord. If we cannot trust the Lord in one another there is no hope. Then we will find that this work is built on me and my ministry and therefore must fail. And I will be the first person to praise God that Halford House has come to an end. I will have no sympathy at all with the older ones who feel that they could say, "I am of Lance. I was with him at the beginning and we went through. When he was with us, we did this and we did that and we did the other." I have no sympathy at all because you should never have been with me, you should have been with the Lord. From the very beginning there were quite a few battles we had, and you older ones knew very well you had to come to the place where you saw my faults but you trusted the Lord in me. So having taken that major step of trusting the Lord in me, you now find it very difficult to trust the Lord in these other brethren—not only the elders but some of the others as well. It is very easy to throw stones. Now I am not saying that anybody is doing that, but as we move ahead, we need the kind of leadership that is going to be in touch with God. And somehow we need to be together so that we can move into all that He has for us in these coming days.

Duties of Elder Brothers

One of the things that I am just going to re-emphasize now is the duties of elder brothers. Their duty is defined here as being overseers to feed the church of the Lord. Now this does not mean that an elder must have a ministry of the Word because in the first letter to Timothy chapter 5:17 it says: "Let the elders that rule well be counted worthy of double honor [double honor meaning good wages], especially those who labor in the Word and in teaching." So evidently there are elders who labor in the Word and in teaching, but not all the elders. The job of the elder is to oversee. They may have other gifts such as a prophetic gift, a counseling gift, a pastor, a teaching ministry, even an evangelistic ministry. However, basically the job of the elder is the overseeing of the whole household of God in a particular area.

Trusting the Lord in the Overseers

Now having said that, what does it mean for overseers to feed the church of God? Does it not mean that their job is to see that the house of God is so functioning that they are being fed. It does not mean that they have to do the feeding, but that the members of the body are feeding one another. Their job is to tend the flock, care for the flock, encourage those who have gifts to exercise them, correct those who are going wrong and be available for counseling where necessary. There will come a time when a lot of our counseling will have to be done by the leaders in the house gatherings because the burden becomes too much for the elders. Then we shall have yet another problem because people who have finally begun to trust the Lord in the elders will now have to take another step and trust the Lord in their group leaders. You see, people cannot trust them. Sometimes we get stuck on what we see and we cannot see the Lord in them. And yet it is an amazing thing that when you trust the Lord in a person you find the Lord. This is unfailing. All of you must have had the experience where you felt you could not go to brother so-and-so about a particular matter, and finally after much hemming and hawing in your heart you took the step of faith and went, and in an amazing way God met you. This is because when we trust the Lord in somebody else, instead of them trying to manipulate us as we think they will or run along some petty line, they themselves come under the government of the Holy Spirit.

Remembering Those Who Have the Rule Over You

In this matter of ruling, the word is very interesting in Hebrews chapter 13. It speaks of remembering them that have the rule over you (v. 7), obey them that have the rule over you (v. 17) salute all them that have the rule over you (v. 24). Overseeing is an interesting function as we find in Hebrews. I like the word because somehow or other it takes out any dictatorship that might be inherent in the word ruling. When we think of a ruler, we think of somebody who says, "Do this! Do that! We shall do this! We shall do that!" And we have to submit to them. But overseeing has a gentler feel about it. And it seems to me that the job of the elders in the church is to see that the rights of God in the people of God are guarded. No matter who or what, that is their first primary job.

The second thing is to see that the house of God is functioning in a healthy manner. I think we have in this company perhaps made some mistakes, for which I take full responsibility, in that we began as a much more centralized company before we broke into house groups. The result was, particularly on Tuesday evening, we sent out all the matters for prayer from a central place because we were so afraid we would lose the character of our prayer life. Looking back as I consider it, it seems to have been a mistake for this reason. It centralized authority in such a way that in our house gatherings we did not seek the Lord as to what we should be praying about and standing together with God for. I do not think there is anything wrong with us as a company as far as life goes. The life is there, the gifts are there, the fullness is there. We have many, many problems like any company, but if somehow we could break through all the things that inhibit us and really stand for God's purpose we could move forward. It is an interesting thing that every time we destroy any sense of a pattern being imposed upon us, there is great life, whether it is in house gatherings or in our own gathering. We just feel the Lord is there. It is a wonderful sense of the Lord being there, of life welling up. And that leads me to this.

It is not the job of the elders to always lead gatherings or in many ways to be too much in the forefront always. Their job is to be there to see that if someone prophesies something which is wrong it should be stopped, that if something is brought in that is erroneous it should be silenced, if there is disorder in the church with ones going hither and there, we are to be there to bring order. But to feel that we have to do all the leading and even administering the Lord's Table all the time, I think it may be a mistake. Our job is the overseeing of the whole and to get the church itself to function. One of the things that we felt would be right would be to detach the elder brethren and the workers from their house groups and let them circulate. We have to find somebody who has a burden to do this. There should be a brother who comes to me or another leading brother and says,

"This Tuesday or this Thursday you are at such and such a group and so-and-so is having you for a meal." Now I have done this for two weeks, and I have had the most marvelous meals. And in the years I have been here I have been in two homes I have never been in before. I sat down, saw the home, heard the problems, saw the children, and of course, I saw God from another angle. Then I went into the gathering and got smothered with kisses because everyone was so amazed to find me in their group. I felt it was very good because probably we brothers tend to inhibit the house gatherings by our presence. Everyone thinks, "Oh, the big brass is here and they know the mind of the Lord for us;" so they do not do anything; we inhibit them. But when we go once in a while to one of the groups, we do not inhibit them. In fact, it becomes an encouragement and people will really function. So I think that is one very good thing that may come out of this. Thus if this can go through, I believe it will be one of the biggest single factors in releasing the life of God amongst us.

Praying Before the Meetings

There is an idea that because we brothers meet before a meeting and pray, we have actually received the whole plan for the meeting. Now there are certain gatherings where we have to do this. We used to do this on Sunday morning in order to find how to begin and we felt basically it should be covered. Now let me say this again—open gatherings of God's people need more spiritual care and oversight than led meetings. When a gathering is organized, it is often one or two people's responsibility to seek the Lord, find the Lord's mind and do it. But when it is an open gathering, there is need behind the scenes to tackle those spiritual forces that would destroy it either by deadness or dullness or heaviness or error or whatever. And that really is the point of some of the brethren getting together before a meeting. It is to cover the time but not to impose a pattern upon it. That should be for the Holy Spirit to bring out of the body. Now if we could get this clear it will, I believe, demolish one or two misconceptions that are prevalent and would make us realize that every one of us is responsible for knowing the mind of the Lord, being led of the Lord and contributing whether in our house gatherings or here. And just because the brothers meet beforehand to cover the time does not mean they have the whole plan for that time. Now I am sure that these brothers, whom we have prayed for, from this time will be freer also. And maybe we shall begin to see a little more clearly that we need to hand things over to the church and be able to say, "We have covered this time, now let us all be together before the Lord to know His will, how we are to move, where we are to go."

The Elders are to Encourage

The job of the elders is to encourage younger brothers, correct them and strengthen them when they lead the gatherings. This is a ministry in which I have perhaps sadly failed in because in the beginning I saw everything and tended towards taking a large part of the central area in leading. By giving this position to other brethren we can see how they are doing, we can strengthen what is of God, and we can perfect what is not.

And in this way we shall begin to go forward. We do not have much time. None of us know how much time we have.

This next world confrontation will come in the end with dramatic suddenness and unexpectedly. Therefore it is incumbent upon us all to really use the time of grace that we have to train one another, to care for one another, and to go forward. So I hope I am making this clear that the brothers' job is counseling and oversight of the assembly, and not substituting themselves for the kind of leadership that God would bring out into the open amongst us; and certainly not to suppress brothers and sisters. I do not believe these brothers, and I know them pretty well, have ever at any single time wanted to suppress the life of God's people. I know them well enough to know that their desire has always been that the life of God should increase and abound more and more. But sometimes unwittingly we do tend to quench the life by somehow, without realizing it is the work of the enemy, there is a feeling of a kind of imposition. And this is what we want to get at and remove so that the life of God amongst us can flow through the members of the body. And the overseers can do the job that God has set them aside to do which is to tend the flock, to give themselves to the real job of counseling, encouraging, correction, and seeing that the house of God is really fed. If these dear brothers are going to feed the house of God, they are going to be dead before long if it is their supreme responsibility and nobody else is included in it. This is not what the Word of God means when it says that the body should increase, building itself up on love.

Those with Wider Responsibility

There is another little point I would like to clear up also in this matter. What is the place of those who have wider responsibilities and local? Some people get very confused here. They feel that a person like myself who was here since the company came into being through my ministry and God-given faith, that therefore he has the supreme responsibility. It is interesting in that letter of 1 Peter 5 he says, "The elders among you I exhort, who am a fellow-elder." This is the apostle Peter and he speaks of himself as a fellow elder. Was he not an apostle at that time? John also in his letter says, "I John, the elder." Was he not an apostle then? In other words, was he an apostle for certain periods of his life and an elder at other periods of his life? Now we do not agree with this system of electing elders or deacons for a three-year run. It does at least give some variety and I suppose that was the idea behind it that you should vote in people for a few years at a time. But I cannot find it in the Word of God that people served a term for two, three or five years. It seems to me that an elder is an elder for life. An apostle is an apostle for life. And I believe that brother Nee did have the key to this matter when he said John was an apostle when he was traveling and he was an elder when he was resident in the local church. And it was the same with Peter. In other words, when he came into the local church, he took his place with the other elders as a fellow elder; but when he went out, he was in apostolic work. And I believe that this will help us greatly in our understanding.

Being Subject to One Another

There is nothing wrong in any of us being subject to other members of the body. The greatest apostle can be at sometimes subject to another. For instance, if I come into your home with your husband, wife, and children and I start throwing my weight around and saying, "We will have tea; China tea." "Oh!" the wife says, "China tea? We have no China tea." "Well, get it then!" "We will not have tea at five; we will have it at six. I am an apostle and I have authority!" This is disorder. Divinely instituted authority in that home is in the hands of the husband and the wife. Do not think the wife has no authority because the Bible says that the wife should rule her household. This is the exact same word as elders ruling the church.

It does not matter whether I am an apostle, an elder, a prophet, a teacher, an evangelist, I have no right to come into your home and disrupt everything. When I am in your home I must be subject to you. If you have Darjeeling, I will have Darjeeling; if you have tea at four-thirty, I will have tea at four-thirty. There is such a thing as authority. In some of these circles there is such a funny idea about authority, such as, the apostle is the absolute all authority in every realm. This is dictatorship. In church history in every one of the circles in which this kind of hierarchy has been introduced, it has ended in disaster because it does not matter who we are, we must be subject to one another. If you have a responsibility given to you from God, I must at least take note of that responsibility. Now if you are not doing it right and I am an elder, I may have to approach you and say, "So-and-so, I do not feel that you are discharging the responsibility God has given you. This matter is very important. That is why I believe it is so good that we brothers could appoint somebody now and again who will tell us which group we are to go to. When I am here, I do not have the responsibility of choosing the group. Otherwise, people would say, "Oh, you are off to Twickenham again, and we know why. You like so-and-so who is there and also so-and-so." It is a good thing to be subject to others who have sought the Lord about the matter. I wish there was a brother or two amongst us who had a real burden about it because it means something to the Lord. This would be a real help in oiling the whole working of the body—ones who would really pray to God and say, "I really feel so-and-so should go to such-and-such a company." The brethren there could sort out who we have a meal with and other things that may arise. I think it is good that we should be subject like this to one another. As the Scripture says, "Subjecting yourselves one to another in the fear of the Lord" (Ephesians 5:21).

Management Problems

Now there is another matter I would like to address. The whole of our country is beset by management problems, and one of the greatest problems is the lack of communication. I think everybody in industry knows that Britain is suffering terribly from a kind of disease. There are those who are employed who cannot trust the manager or the manager class, and then there are those who are in the employer class who cannot trust the employee. And it seems to me that this spirit is also very much in the church. It is a kind of antigovernment or antiauthority thing—"Ah, the elders!"

One of the sisters has told us one or two dreadful stories culled from the depths of Ethiopia at various times. The story is of a very wealthy lady who built a church with all the modern conveniences. When I say "built a church" I mean the building. And when the vicar arrived he was a bit surprised to find that there was only one pew in this vast marvelous building, and it was at the back. So he wondered where everybody was going to sit. As they came in the ushers would take the people to the pew to be seated. As soon as it was filled, they pressed a button and it slid to the front and another one came up out of the floor. They filled the next pew, pressed the button, and it slid up to the front with them. So there were no people sitting in the back. Everybody who came in thought they were going to sit in the back, but they were moved to the front. The clergy thought that this was a marvelous idea! The place was packed, and the vicar got into the pulpit to preach. When it got to twelve o'clock, suddenly the pulpit disappeared into the floor. Someone else had pressed another button and got rid of the clergy.

Problems in the Church

Now this is a funny story but it does go to the root of a problem that those with responsibility and leadership often have very real problems with a company of believers. People will not take responsibility and if they do they are nervous and often stay at the back. If we can only get them forward. Thank God for any answer we had to get them into the front, get them sort of involved. But then the company often have a problem with the leadership, and there are times when they would love to shut them up.

They would love to press a button and get them to disappear into the floor. These problems are not enormous but we do have a certain amount of them where we feel the leadership is either dull or not clear enough or it is not bold enough or it is not definite enough. We sometimes feel they say too much and we could do without it. Or they do not say enough where we could do with a little more information. Let us face the fact that those with responsibility of leadership have very real problems with the people of God. People say, "Why do we always have to do what the leaders say?" The leaders give responsibility and people do not turn up. They share more and they find that the people who were the first to say, "We need to be trained," just do not come. Then it falls back on the old faithful ones. Now if we are really going to go forward, it is no good pitch-forking blame onto one another by either saying it is either this or that or the other. I have to face my own problems in myself. And really what it comes down to is laying down our life for the Lord and for His people, and if we are not prepared for that and for the discipline that is involved and everything else that will come with it, we are not going to go forward. However if we are prepared for that, I believe that God has very much ahead for us in this part of His family.

The Beginning Stage of the House Church

We were in the vanguard of this whole movement that is called the house church. It was by the grace of God and the ordination of God alone and had nothing to do with either me or with us. When we began it was a long and lonely and bitter fight. We were totally misunderstood, people would not come to us, they would not touch us, but through the years God gave us prayer ministry as well as teaching ministry. And in the sixties a miracle happened and all over the world what God had said to us from the beginning happened. Though what He said, "I will keep you small," happened. We are not saying that we are responsible for it because the Lord was responsible for it. But we can say that by His grace we were involved in some small part in it. And the prayer battle was the biggest thing of all. Now today we do not have those same problems. Everywhere we go all over the world people talk about the church, the body, the gifts, building one another up, belonging to one another, being built together. Twenty years ago if you talked about these things people's mouths dropped open, and they thought, "What kind of Christian nut case are you?" Now everybody understands. I will not say all the practice is good, that there is not excess, that there are not problems, that there is not controversy, that there is not much error, but the whole atmosphere has totally changed from one where the thing was just not understood into something which the Lord has done through the work of the Holy Spirit.

The Days that Lie Ahead

Now I do not feel that our calling as a company of God's people is over. We have a job to do in being able to show other groups such as ourselves, who are much younger than us, that we can be built together, that we can function together, that we do not have to just endlessly sing, but there can be all the other contributions that are mentioned in the Word of God, so that there is a healthy, full balance in the house of God. This I believe is something we have yet to give. I believe too that we have some connection or part to play with the Jewish people and with Israel. Now this may be more my part than yours, but I have a feeling it will involve all of you as well. Therefore, at present I am taken out of the way as far as you are concerned and have to be for a while. And though at times I would long to come back, I feel it will damage what the Lord is seeking to do with you as a company getting your feet solidly on the foundation with each one bolted together horizontally like the boards of the tabernacle. When God has done this work, maybe we shall enter into a new phase as a church which has a corporate teaching ministry and not just mine. One of the greatest needs now is going to be the training of men who can minister the Word of God and men who can shoulder the responsibilities in the household of God in the years that lie ahead. If I am right in this matter, I would not be at all surprised if in our lifetime there is a huge world confrontation and bust up with super powers and destruction of the Soviet system, a devastation of the capitalist system, with the world left in a moral, political and economic vacuum for something like five, six, seven years. This will be the greatest opportunity (if I am right) that the church of God has had to evangelize since Pentecost. And in that moral vacuum we have got to be ready, not just here, but the people of God everywhere. Because at the end of that the antichrist will come and with him that system which will usher in the last phase of world history. Of course, this is speculation.

Not By Might Nor By Power,
But By My Spirit, Saith the Lord

That means that all us should have a sense of destiny and a sense of calling. Our horizons are not just, "Oh, we are at Halford House; it is all dreadfully dull and routine, that dreadful house gathering I have to trot off to whenever they meet." We have to go and we have to contribute. Every one of us has our part to play to be trained in the time that we have left to us. We have this little time left to us whether we are young in the Lord or whether we are old in the Lord. You older ones, please seek to help. I know you all well. We have battled together, we have fought together, we have stuck together, which is the biggest miracle, for twenty-seven years. There are times when we have seen right through one another and still stayed together. Do not paralyze what God is seeking to do. Do not always be harking back to the good old days. Look to God because we have time in which He is going to train us, to qualify us for what lies ahead. I am quite sure that this is the reason why today the Lord has led us to this simple little act of setting aside our brethren for elder-hood leadership. And I think now we should sing "Not By Might Nor By Power" and then go to the Lord in prayer. Let us take this whole thing back to the Lord and cover these brethren. Let us ask the Lord to anoint them in a way they have never been anointed before. Let us ask the Lord to demolish those bondages in conception or mind which hold some back from functioning and let us ask the Lord that they may be enabled to really give themselves to what God has for them.

Now we have not mentioned the group leaders because we feel that it would be premature to take all the group leaders and set them aside at this time. We feel we should leave it just a little longer; but these dear brethren have an even greater problem. If folks feel that the elders are not Lance, I am quite sure when you get to the group leaders they will say, "Oh, they are not the elders." You cannot exercise authority unless people let you. Never forget, you cannot exercise authority unless people let you. Let us sing, "Not by Might, Nor by Power, but by My Spirit, saith the Lord."

7.
True Authority

Mark 10:35-45

And there come near unto him James and John, the sons of Zebedee, saying unto him, Teacher, we would that thou shouldest do for us whatsoever we shall ask of thee. And he said unto them, What would ye that I should do for you? And they said unto him, Grant unto us that we may sit, one on thy right hand, and one on thy left hand, in thy glory. But Jesus said unto them, Ye know not what ye ask. Are ye able to drink the cup that I drink? or to be baptized with the baptism that I am baptized with? And they said unto him, We are able. And Jesus said unto them, The cup that I drink ye shall drink; and with the baptism that I am baptized withal shall ye be baptized: but to sit on my right hand or on my left hand is not mine to give; but it is for them for whom it hath been prepared. And when the ten heard it, they began to be moved with indignation concerning James and John. And Jesus called them to him, and saith unto them,

Ye know that they who are accounted to rule over the Gentiles lord it over them; and their great ones exercise authority over them. But it is not so among you: but whosoever would become great among you, shall be your minister, and whosoever would be first among you, shall be servant [or bond slave] of all. For the Son of man also came not to be ministered unto, but to minister, and to give his life a ransom for many.

I want to share with you on this matter of authority—true authority. We are living in days which have been described as a crisis of authority and the spirit of rebellion, of anarchy, of license is apparent everywhere. It is not only in our educational system, it is not only in our national and social life, it has not only reached into family life, but the spirit of it has come into the church. And so this matter of authority is all important.

Now this would be a happy matter if there was not a tremendous amount of problem and confusion on this very subject amongst believers, and not least amongst those who are most desirous of seeing the Lord recover His testimony and build His church. We see in many, many movements, that have some measure of real church truth, a confusion on the matter of authority, perhaps not so much in teaching as in practice. The end result is that empires are built, human systems are created, a kind of Christian spiritual police state is somehow produced, a system of bondage is imposed upon the people of God. This matter therefore of authority is vital. It goes to the very heart of everything.

Authority in Leadership

As we are considering this matter of leadership, we know that there can be no leadership without authority. And I am not just talking about apostolic work or the work of an elder, the work of some responsible brother who is leading or with others leading an assembly of God's people. I am talking about those of you who are responsible for children's work or youth work or for some practical aspect of the life of God's people. Leadership goes right through the whole church of God. If you have a responsibility, however small it might be in some measure, it is a matter of leadership. However small the responsibility delegated to you, it is to be seen in terms of leadership. So what I have to say has a very wide scope and bearing. It is not just for those who occupy the platform, those who are forever in evidence as leading meetings or whatever else. It goes into every aspect of our life as the people of God.

The Nature of True Authority

Now the first thing I would like to underline is the nature of true authority. All true authority is derived from God. It is not self-made self-appointed; it cannot be. This is apparent in the fact that the apostle Paul again and again opened his letters by saying, "Paul, an apostle of Jesus Christ by the will of God." And in the Galatian letter he says, "Paul, an apostle of Jesus Christ, not by men, but through God." Therefore all true authority must have as its source the appointment of God.

Now this is true even of the world. What does the Bible teach us about, for instance, your President, whether you like him or not, about our Prime Minister in England or other world leaders? It is quite clear in Romans 13:

Let every soul be in subjection to the higher powers:
for there is no power (or authority) but of God;
and the powers that be are ordained of God.
Therefore he that resisteth authority, withstandeth the
ordinance of God: and they that withstand shall
receive to themselves judgment
Romans 13:1–2

In the first letter of Peter it says this:

"Be subject to every ordinance of man for the Lord's sake:
whether to the king, as supreme; or unto governors,
as sent by him for vengeance on evil-doers and for praise to
them that do well. For so is the will of God, that by well-doing
ye should put to silence the ignorance of foolish men:
as free, (that is you are above actual human authority
in this fallen world) and not using your freedom for a cloak
of wickedness, but as bond slaves of God. Honor all men.
Love the brotherhood. Fear God. Honor the king"
1 Peter 2:13–17

Spiritual Authority is from the Lord

Now if, in fact, even authority in a fallen world is appointed by God, how much more must authority in the work of God and in the church of God be appointed by the Lord? All spiritual authority is derived from the Lord. Let me underline it again and again. Look for instance at Matthew 28 and those very well-known words:

> And Jesus came to them and spake unto them, saying,
> "All authority hath been given unto me in heaven and on
> earth. Go ye therefore, and make disciples of all the nations,
> baptizing them into the name of the Father and of the Son
> and of the Holy Spirit: teaching them to observe all things
> whatsoever I commanded you: and lo, I am with you always,
> even unto the end of the world (or the end of the age)"
> Matthew 28:18–20

"All authority and power is given unto Me, go ye therefore." Our authority in the work of God is derived from His authority. Now this matter is very, very important because it is not merely a matter of title or status or position or dress or training or academic qualification or election to office. These things may be right or they may be wrong. You can make a person a "reverend," but he may not be reverent. You can give a theological degree to somebody who does not have the faintest understanding of spiritual things and does not know what it is to live in a spiritual dimension. Such authority is the authority of this world. It is dependent upon dress, upon title, upon status, upon some kind of academic qualification. Now this is not to run down academic qualifications or training, it is not even to take away title; after all the apostle Paul called himself the apostle Paul and was not afraid to talk about elders and deacons in the early church. But if we think that it is merely a question that we can "elderize" a man or "deaconize" a man or "preacherize" a man or "apostlize" a man or produce people to be things, you are very, very wrong. All those matters are secondary. The ordination in its first place to any responsibility in the work of God must be the Lord.

Now this does not mean the church may not at times come to you and ask you to do a job, because behind the burden of the church or behind the burden of those responsible brethren may in fact be the voice and appointment of God. But the point I am trying to make is simply this: that all real authority comes from the Lord, and we must be appointed by God. Otherwise, we shall forever have a kind of nagging suspicion that we are in the wrong place, and we do not have that divine support, that divine backing, that divine covering, that divine provision.

The Lord Jesus was under Authority

Now I would like to take this matter a step further. I would like you to note the words of the centurion to the Lord Jesus as recorded in the gospel of Luke: "And Jesus went with them. And when he was now not far from the house, the centurion sent friends to him, saying unto him, Lord, trouble not thyself; for I am not worthy that thou shouldest come under my roof: wherefore neither thought I myself worthy to come unto thee: but say the word, and my servant shall be healed. For I also am a man set under authority, having under myself soldiers: and I say to this one, Go, and he goeth; and to another, Come, and he cometh; and to my servant, Do this, and he doeth it" (Luke 7:6–8).

Now I want you just to note these words of the centurion to the Lord Jesus: "I also am under authority." The Lord Jesus was also under authority. Consider very carefully what the Lord Jesus said in John 5 because in hearing the words of the Lord Jesus we come right through to this matter more clearly. I want to just lay a foundation first of all before I talk about the character of authority. "Jesus therefore answered and said unto them: 'Verily, verily, I say unto you, The Son can do nothing of himself, but what He seeth the Father doing: for what things soever He doeth, these the Son also doeth in like manner'" (John 5:19).

What mysterious words—the Son can do nothing of (or from) himself, but what He seeth the Father doing. The Father in Him is doing the work. The Father in him is the authority. In the same chapter are these words: "For as the Father hath life in himself, even so gave he to the Son also to have life in himself: and He gave Him authority to execute judgment, because He is a Son of man (that is Messiah)" (John 5:26–27). "I can of myself do nothing: as I hear, I judge: and my judgment is righteous; because I seek not mine own will, but the will of him that sent me" (v. 30).

True Authority

Now here you have the nature of true authority— "I seek not my own will but the will of Him that sent me." So true authority is first of all God Himself. He is the only authority, and all other authority is derived. We are servants, and we are not out to do our own will; we are only out to administer His will.

Maybe this all seems to you very "kindergarten," very obvious and so on, but in fact it goes to the root of all our problems. We have thousands of brethren throwing their weight around in the house of God, lording it over the flock, somehow or other trying to be something. It becomes a platform for ambition, a platform for self-expression, a platform for self-assertion. It becomes a little petty empire in which small men can become big dictators. This is not authority; it is a travesty of authority. Real authority is when you have a man or a woman who can do nothing from themselves. That does not mean they are continually self-conscious, tied up—no, no, they are the freest of all people. But they cannot judge of themselves and they cannot exercise authority of themselves and they cannot rule of themselves. It has to be the Lord in them. It is so important.

The Need for Brokenness

No servant of the Lord can ever experience these words of the Lord Jesus in his or her experience until he knows brokenness, until he has gone through that process whereby God in His infinite grace and mercy breaks him of the strength of his own will and the strength of his own emotion and the strength of his own concepts. When God has broken a man or a woman, then they can become a vehicle of authority. It is the principle of the cross and the Spirit. A man must learn to die; a woman must learn to die. They must know what it is in a cold-blooded way to lay down their lives for the sake of the Lord and the for the sake of His church, His body, and for the sake of the world. Then the Spirit of God comes upon them and the authority of God is manifested.

Now maybe you feel I am setting such a standard that everyone will say, "We better all resign from the various responsibilities we have. This is dreadful. Does he really mean to say that my little Sunday school job, my looking after the kids has got to be derived authority?" But in actual fact, yes, because if those children are to become the recipients of the Word of God, if some impression is to be made upon their little hearts and minds in their earliest years you have to be gotten out of the way so that the Lord can come through you, not apart from you. There is this idea of sanctification that God ties us up in a knot, smashes us over the head with a ten pound hammer, then kicks us out and stands there Himself. But this is not sanctification. God takes a Paul with a brain—one of the greatest brains in the world—then He breaks the man not once, but again and again, and then He comes through the brain. Do not think that God does not use intelligence. He does use intelligence, and He sometimes uses dimness. This is no commendation—Balaam's ass once prophesied and there have been many ever since!

Temperament is temperament. God knows exactly what He is doing because He says in one place: "When you were in your mother's womb I formed you" (Jeremiah 1:5). In other words, your genetic history is under the government of God. And if you have a strong will, then I can tell you that if you are going to be called by God and appointed by God to some sphere of leadership, you have a very real period of anguish to pass through because God has to break you first so that His work will not be scarred or marred by the wrong kind of authority.

Broken at the Sight of the Lord

I mentioned that the apostle Paul was a man with an incredible brain. Some have called him a man with a brain as great as any in the history of the world. Maybe this is true, maybe it is overstating the case. Certainly I think we all must agree (I have to meet him one day so I have to be careful what I say) that the apostle Paul had above average intelligence and brain. And God broke him in the vision that came to him that blinded him for three days. Like a little child the great Paul had to be led to some unknown man that we would not even know his name if it were not for Paul, called Annanias, who laid hands on the great man and prayed for him. We do not really know what happened to Paul when he was in the desert for three years, but we do know that after there had been given to him revelation after revelation and responsibility for the churches of God and for the work of God over a very wide area, God gave him a thorn in the flesh, a messenger from Satan that he might not be exalted over much (II Corinthians 12:7).

We must thank God if we do not have such a thorn in the flesh, but the principle remains true relatively of all servants of the Lord. The more revelation that is given to them, the deeper the experience and the greater their vision of God, the more God takes measures to keep them small and broken. This matter of true authority therefore is no easy matter. If we aspire to leadership, if we want to be at least responsible in the work of God in these days, I think the matter of leadership is one of the most important and essential matters in the whole work of God.

As a Little Child

Let us consider the character of true authority. It is seen in a number of places but I want to dwell on two in particular in the Gospel according to Mark. And we expect to find it in this Gospel because this is all to do with service and Jesus as the Servant of the Lord:

> And they came to Capernaum: and when he was in the
> house he asked them, What were ye reasoning on the way?
> But they held their peace: for they had disputed one with
> another on the way, who was the greatest. And he sat down,
> and called the twelve; and he saith unto them, If any man
> would be first, he shall be last of all, and servant
> [or bond slave] of all. And he took a little child, and set him
> in the midst of them: and taking him in his arms, he said unto
> them, Whosoever shall receive one of such little children
> in my name, receiveth me: and whosoever receiveth me,
> receiveth not me, but him that sent me
> Mark 9:33–37

What really was the Lord saying or meaning in this statement or in this act? Was He saying that whoever would be first, whoever would be greatest must become like a little child? What did He mean when He said whoever receives Him receives Him that sent Him? In other words, the Lord Jesus may have been talking about His servants. These twelve were His disciples and what He was really saying was this: "You have got to become like a little child, dependent upon God, pure in heart, if you would really know the authority of God and the greatness of God, if you would be first." That is one way of looking at it. I think it is a legitimate way.

But another way to look at it is this way. The servant of the Lord who becomes big will often overlook little people. And very often it has pleased God to say something through little people. It is not always where we expect to hear God speak that we hear Him speak. The two things come together. Unless we are small in our own heart and estimation, unless we are dependent upon God, unless we are pure in heart, I do not know whether we would ever be ready to listen to God speaking through some non-entity. What can a child do in the house of God? What great work can they do? What great sign can they work? What great wonder can they perform? What great prophecy can they make? What great mystery can they explain? What great faith can they exercise? Yet sometimes God takes the humblest person in the assembly and reveals to them a key to a whole problem confronting that work. But leaders sometimes get so big and leadership can be so locked into itself that it cannot hear what God is trying to say through the body.

In Mark 10 Jesus says: "Ye know that they who are accounted to rule over the Gentiles lord it over them; and their great ones exercise authority over them. But it is not so among you: but whosoever would become great among you, shall be your servant; and whosoever would be first among you, shall be bond slave of all" (vv. 42–44).

The First Shall Be the Bondslave of All

"Whoever shall be great among you shall be servant" is the lower level. The servant was a hired servant, not quite the same as a bond slave. A bond slave was at the beck and call of the household twenty-four hours. The hired servant not only had hours of service but he also had wages. The bond slave had no wages; he was kept. Even his wife and children belonged to the master.

What does the Lord Jesus say? "You know that amongst the Gentiles how their great ones like to lord it over them but it shall not be so amongst you. But whosoever shall be great shall be like a hired servant. But whoever would be first shall be bond slave of all." Would to God we all had that kind of character. If all authority exercised in the work of God and in the church of God was of this character, of this type, what a tremendous difference it would make in the work of the Lord. Have we given sufficient value to the words of our Lord Jesus? He went on to say this in verse 45: "For the Son of man also came not to be ministered unto, but to minister, and to give his life a ransom for many." This is the character of true authority.

God's Idea of Kingship

Do you not think that the enemy has done his most cunning and most deceitful work in this matter of leadership in somehow causing the very atmosphere of our assemblies, of our fellowships, of churches, of Christian work amongst the people of God to be permeated by this idea that is in the world? The man who is the leader is the big man. He has a Cadillac, and he just lounges back. He is driven here or driven there. He has a big office. When you come in, you stand there, and it is "Yes sir, no sir, please sir." We get this idea of kingship which is of someone sitting, as it were, on a magnificent gold throne with a wonderful crown and all the regalia of that office. It is something that makes your mouth just drop open when you see it, "Oh, how wonderful!" Even our idea of the kingship of Jesus falls into this category. We often just think of him sitting on the throne to be admired, as if the Lord Jesus wants to be admired. As if the only reason for saving us is that He might sit there and everyone sort of say "Ooh." This is not kingship. God's idea of kingship is service. It is to be the bond slave of all. It is to be at the beck and call of all. We see it in Jesus if we do not see it in one another, if you do not see it in me.

This matter is not very easy. The Lord Jesus was truly the bond slave of all. He fed them, He loved them, He healed them from early morning to late at night and then would not send them away. What a picture of authority we see in the Lord Jesus, the One who could quell a storm, the One who could cast out a legion of demons, the One who could raise the dead, the One who could heal the sick, the One Who could give the mentally ill a sound mind. This Jesus never threw His weight around; He was the bond slave of all. He thought about feeding them. He thought about caring for them. He worried about their condition. He knew what was happening when some dear little shriveled-up lady in her old age touched the hem of His garment. He knew it. Virtue went out of Him, He said. Even when He faced the greatest trial of His life, He took a towel and girded Himself with it and took a basin of water and washed the feet of His disciples. He knelt in front of them, the very men who were going to deny Him within hours, and Judas who was going out to betray Him and sell Him, He knelt before him and washed his feet.

This is a picture of authority which is entirely foreign to us. Our idea of authority is as I have said before like a pyramid structure. It is often drawn as a pyramid. You have got the apostles at the top and under those you have the prophets and under that you have the elders and under that you have the deacons and under that you have the mass of the church. The apostle having the greatest authority sits as it were, on the top. Now there is nothing wrong about this idea because if you look at the Word it often says "Firstly apostles, then prophets ..." (1 Corinthians 12:28), so we get this idea: "Well of course, firstly apostles, then prophets, then pastors, teachers, evangelists." Then we go on down to the serried ranks until finally you come to poor little you and me squashed at the bottom. In one sense, there is nothing wrong with it but I always say it is best to invert the pyramid because it is the concept that does the damage. It is not the truth, it is the concept. You see, concepts govern behavior. When you have this idea of the apostles as the big boys at the top, and all the poor folks, who are the redeemed, underneath them, it is a concept. Therefore anyone who aspires to leadership is thinking of going up the ladder. "We are going up. We are going to be something! We are going to be able to exercise authority!"

We must invert the pyramid. It says in Ephesians 2:20: "Being built upon the foundation of the apostles and prophets, Christ Jesus himself being the chief corner stone." In other words, if we invert the whole pyramid the whole weight comes down upon those with the greatest authority, and everything is focused with them in burden, in anguish, in suffering, in travail. And is it not so when we read the New Testament?

A Caution on Purpose for Service

This will help us to understand this matter a little more when we read 1 Peter 5: "Tend the flock of God [he is speaking to elders] which is among you, exercising the oversight, not of constraint, but willingly, according to the will of God; nor yet for filthy lucre, but of a ready mind; neither as lording it over the charge allotted to you, but making yourselves examples to the flock" (vv. 2–3).

This is how the New American Standard Bible puts it: "Not under compulsion, but voluntarily, according to the will of God; and not for sordid gain, (Now that does not just mean money. Sordid gain can be ambition. It can be self-fulfillment. It can be self-expression. It can be a satisfaction of one's own ego.) but with eagerness." So we are not to be those people who say, "Oh, no, no, I cannot do anything." We have to be sort of driven into it. No. "Not of compulsion, but with eagerness." Do you see the paradox? We are eager to lead the people of God. What does it mean? If I am right, it means you are eager for suffering, you are eager for burden, you are eager for anguish, you are eager for criticism, you are eager for all the many things that will come your way, including in some cases a messenger of Satan. Do not be compelled out of duty to take responsibility in the work of God, but do it eagerly because you want to follow your Lord and you want to come to the throne of God by His grace.

Examples to the Flock

"Nor yet as lording it over those allotted to your charge, but proving to be examples." Examples! What are examples if they are not pioneers? We are not to lord it over the people of God but we are to lead them. We are to pioneer the way first in prayer. I do not mean in opening our mouth, but always if there is a time of prayer we are there. Where are our leaders often? There is a time of prayer—not there. There is a night of prayer, they are not there. They are too busy. We cannot expect everybody else to give up a night if we do not give up a night. We cannot expect others to sacrifice unless we sacrifice ourselves. We cannot expect people to give their time and money and energy unless we do. We must be first in this matter. We must be pioneers in this matter. Not directing things from behind the lines far back in the safety of the capital, but out in front in the war leading the people, not lording it over the flock allotted to you but as examples.

Exercising Authority

Now I want to say something about the exercise of authority, this most ticklish of all matters. These are the words of the apostle Paul in II Timothy 4: "Give diligence to come shortly unto me: for Demas forsook me, having loved this present world, and went to Thessalonica; Crescens to Galatia, Titus to Dalmatia. Only Luke is with me. Take Mark, and bring him with thee; for he is useful to me for ministering. But Tychicus I sent to Ephesus" (vv. 9–12).

This is interesting. He sent Tychicus to Ephesus, but the rest departed. Now there is no word of condemnation for Titus or Crescens. It says expressly that Demas forsook Paul having loved this present world. What an interesting window into the whole matter of authority. One would have thought that the apostle Paul would have been bull-headed in authority, maybe saying to Crescens: "You cannot go! I need you here! The testimony of the Lord needs you here. I have to face one of the biggest shows of satanic strength that I have ever faced. You must stay with me." But he did not. If Crescens wants to go, he can go. If Titus wants to go, he lets him go. Luke stayed with him, and he sent Tychicus to

Ephesus. How interesting. Now it is not that it was wrong for Titus to go to Dalmatia. Maybe it was right, but the way the apostle Paul writes it, it seems that it was without his fellowship.

How do we exercise authority? Look at verses 20–21a: "Erastus remained at Corinth: but Trophimus I left at Miletus sick. Give diligence to come before winter."

Now we have to put this little window into the exercise of authority in the ministry and life of the apostle Paul over against those other things when he speaks, for instance, in Corinth when he used the authority which he had and said, "Many of you will be sorry." Even there we have a very interesting thing as we find in II Corinthians 10: "For though I should glory somewhat abundantly concerning our authority (which the Lord gave for building you up, and not for casting you down), I shall not be put to shame: that I may not seem as if I would terrify you by my letters. For, His letters, they say, are weighty and strong; but his bodily presence is weak, and his speech of no account" (vv. 8–10).

That is a very interesting window upon the exercising of authority. Evidently when the apostle Paul wrote letters, it was tremendous, but when he was there, he did not give the impression of being a tremendous authority. He spoke about the signs which he worked and the wonders which he performed. He said that it is not in word, but in deed (10:11). But what an interesting window into this matter of the exercising of authority. Let me say two things about it.

The Way of the Cross

Firstly, there are times when your exercising of authority is the way of the cross. When sometimes you have to stand up and withstand somebody or rebuke somebody, sometimes it is the way of the cross. It would be easier to say nothing, easier for peace to be quiet. But if God has appointed you and given you responsibility and He touches your responsibility, you may have to speak or you will come into collision with your Lord. That authority which He has given you is not yours; it is His. And if anyone wants to rebel against it or contradict it, the Lord will take them on. For some of us it is the hardest thing when we have been dealt with by God and gone through something of His mill to speak up and say something, to rebuke, to correct.

There are other times when the way of the cross is to let go. When someone charges you with something or accuses you of something personal or points out all your failings and mistakes, there is a time just to let go and die. It is the distinguishing of these two things that is vital in the work of God—when to stand up and say something, when to rebuke, and when to die.

Not Mastering People

The other thing I would like to say is this: For all of you who are leaders or have any responsibility for other lives, never master those allotted to your care. What do I mean? All of life is the mastering of people. Business is built on it. You have to master them, you have to possess them, you have to get on top of them. That is the way the world rules. You have to somehow inhibit them. You have to put fear into them. You have to put a mystique around yourself in order to regulate them or govern them. This is not the way of spiritual authority. We do great damage to one another when we master one another. It is very easy when you have authority in the work of God to say to someone,

"You shall do this, you shall not do that. You shall go here; you shall not go there." However, there is a place where we must say what we have to say, but we must never master people. When I say that you must never master those who are allotted to your charge, I am not thinking of Sunday school children or youth work. I am thinking in connection of adults. It is very easy to abuse authority and so to substitute yourself, your history and your life, your experience in the place of original experience and original appreciation of the Lord in the person who is your responsibility. And that is something you and I have to be very careful about. That is why I personally would never exercise authority over any brother or brethren unless they first came and asked me and I felt that they were at a place where it would not damage them. We do great damage to one another when we master one another, and we inhibit one another from growing up. Now this is a very delicate matter and we could take a lot more time to talk about it, but I just wanted to clear that up.

Authority under Authority

I have felt myself (and I may be wrong) that the way God would have authority exercised is when we are all in some way under authority. In other words, I do not think any child of God can exercise authority until they have been under authority, and have been in a very rigid school of discipline. How are we going to do this? I remember when I was much younger in the Lord and I came up against this thing, and I felt that the Lord would have me go to Mr. Sparks. I was not in that assembly. In fact I lived quite far from it. We had our own work which had been indigenous altogether apart from that work at Honor Oak, as it was called.

But I felt I had to go and say to him, "I want to submit myself." And there were people who came and warned me. They said, "Don't do it, don't do it; he will destroy you. He will ruin you." Now Mr. Sparks, for those of you who knew him, was a man of supreme authority. He only had to look at you and you could quiver. He was a man of few words. But I felt I had to do it, so I went. And the first thing he said to me was this, "You shall baptize nobody." Now that was particularly hard because we were going to baptize some people the next week. He also said, "You shall marry nobody" (to clarify, Mr. Sparks did not tell me that I should not marry personally; he told me that I should not perform marriages). That was another blow. And then thoughts came to me: "How right is this? This is another assembly; what right has another assembly to have anything to do with me?" But then I remember what God had said to me, and in the end everything came back to me. I was so thankful for it. I learned more by submitting to him than I have ever learned from anybody else. I was not unaware of our dear beloved brother's failings or weaknesses. But he never interrogated me. He never said, "Why are you doing this or this?" or "this is wrong." But I would go to him and say, "Is there anything that you see that is wrong?" And he would say, "Yes." But he did not master me.

Now I do not want in any way to destroy or ruin or mar the reputation of that great servant of the Lord through whom we have learned so much. But there were those who were marred by Mr. Sparks because their attitude to his authority was wrong. They were mastered by it. When you open up yourself in a right way spiritually to another brother, you do not have any bitterness in your heart. If when you go to a brother and say, "Tell me;

is there anything you see in my spirit or my behavior that is wrong? Just tell me." When that brother says, "Well, there is this and this," you do not feel bitter because you yourself have opened up to him.

Now I know there is an awful lot of talk about authority and submission, and I fear that in some cases it is like a police state. Yet there is such a thing as authority and there is such a thing as submission. But it is the spiritual nature of it that is so important. May God help us in all these things. I am very conscious of taking a matter like this of such tremendous importance and just outlining a few things and leave many other things unsaid. But if I can leave you with anything it must be this: If you are going to lead, you yourself must be led. And you must be led first and foremost by the Lord. If you are going to be responsible for other human lives and care for them, you must know what it is to be under the care of somebody else for a while, and you must learn what that discipline is. It is not something that is harshly imposed upon you like a police state but something which you willingly open yourself up to. May God preserve us from the dangers and may He lead us into the reality because there could be no more wonderful thing than if the authority of our Lord was to be manifested in the house of God throughout the United States and Canada and indeed through the nations of the world in these days. May He help us.

8.
The Necessity
of Anointing

Romans 15:17–20

I have therefore my glorying in Christ Jesus in things pertaining to God. For I will not dare to speak of any things save those which Christ wrought through me, for the obedience of the Gentiles, by word and deed, in the power of signs and wonders, in the power of the Holy Spirit; so that from Jerusalem, and round about even unto Illyricum, I have fully preached the gospel of Christ; yea, making it my aim so to preach the gospel, not where Christ was already named, that I might not build upon another man's foundation.

1 Corinthians 2:1–5

And I, brethren, when I came unto you, came not with excellency of speech or of wisdom, proclaiming to you the testimony of God. For I determined not to know anything among you, save Jesus Christ, and him crucified. And I was with you in weakness, and in fear, and in much trembling.

And my speech and my
preaching were not in
persuasive words of wisdom,
but in demonstration of

the Spirit and of power:
that your faith should not
stand in the wisdom of men,
but in the power of God.

Underline in this scripture these words: In Romans 15:18 he speaks about those things which Christ wrought through me, in the power of the Holy Spirit. He also speaks of "by word and deed, in the power of signs and wonders, in the power of the Holy Spirit."

1 Corinthians 2:4–5

And my speech and my
preaching were not in
persuasive words of wisdom,
but in demonstration of the
Spirit and of power:
that your faith should not
stand in the wisdom of men,
but in the power of God.

1 Thessalonians 1:5

...how that our gospel came not
unto you in word only, but also
in power, and in the Holy Spirit,
and in much assurance; even as
ye know what manner of men
we showed ourselves toward
you for your sake.

Set Apart and Anointed

Now I would like to introduce the subject of anointing or the necessity of anointing, and I am aware that we cannot deal with it adequately. The first thing I would like to say straightaway is that it is a most remarkable fact that in the Old Testament every single thing or person that God ever used was anointed. In other words, under the Old Covenant, from the moment God had a people, everything that was set aside for Him was anointed. The high priest (Exodus 29:29; 28:41); the king or the kings (1 Samuel 10:1); the prophet (1 Kings 19:16 or Psalm 105:15) were all anointed and used by God.

Then every single thing in the tabernacle was anointed. The furniture of the tent of meeting, the lampstand, the showbread table, the golden altar of incense, the actual tent of meeting itself, the brazen altar and the laver were all anointed (Exodus 30:26–28). So this must have some very real and important meaning for us all. Why did God go to such bother not only that everything was sprinkled with blood but everything was anointed with the holy anointing oil?

Then I would like to underline another very instructive fact. The very term Messiah in Hebrew, Mashiach, means "Anointed One," and we use the anglicized Greek, (which I have always been rather sorry for), from the New Testament: Christ from the Greek or Christos and the anglicized Greek word means what the Hebrew means; it is the equivalent of the Hebrew. It means the Anointed One. The Messiah was the Anointed One. And I think that is very, very important especially when you understand that we find a little phrase that runs right through the New Testament in connection with every single aspect of our salvation, of our Christian life, of church life and of service to God. It is a little phrase of two words: in Christ. And that simply means that every true believer, every born again believer is in the Anointed One.

That is thier position. They are in the One who is anointed. Now it seems a very odd thing to me that you can be in the Anointed One and be ignorant of the anointing, to be in the Anointed One and never come to your own experience of what it is to be anointed.

Born of the Spirit

Another very instructive and fundamental fact is that the Lord Jesus was born of the Spirit, and we know this from the Gospel according to Luke and other Scriptures. The Holy Spirit dwelt in the Lord Jesus as He had never dwelt in any other human being. As a man, altogether apart from His divinity, the Holy Spirit dwelt in the Lord Jesus. I cannot conceive of any time in the life of the Lord Jesus when He was not full of the Spirit, when He was not indwelt by the Spirit. He was born of the Spirit, but when He was thirty years of age, the year when the Levite or priest entered into his actual service, he was anointed with the Holy Spirit and with power. You will remember that He went down into the Jordan River, and there as He was being baptized the heavens opened and the Holy Spirit came down like a dove and abode upon Him. It did not just visit Him, it did not just use Him, it did not inspire Him; the Holy Spirit came down and took up His dwelling place, His abode, in and upon the Lord Jesus.

In Acts 10 we read a very interesting comment by one of the apostles when speaking of the Lord Jesus: "Even Jesus of Nazareth, how God anointed him with the Holy Spirit and with power: who went about doing good, and healing all that were oppressed of the devil; for God was with him" (Acts 10:38).

Now this is interesting because it does not mean that God was with Him in a kind of supportive way but that God had committed Himself totally to Him as the Son of man. That anointing was the committal of God to the Lord Jesus totally for His ministry and for His work. Now if this is so for us, as servants of the Lord, it has tremendous value. It is tremendously important because we may be born of the Holy Spirit, we may walk in the Spirit, we may know what it is to be indwelt by the Spirit, we may have the fruit of the Spirit, but we need the anointing of the Spirit for service.

Now if anyone has a problem over this, I do not want to argue about it. If you feel that everything is yours at birth, I am not going to argue with you. Maybe it is true and if you are satisfied with the quality of your service and the power with which you are serving the Lord and the ability with which you are fulfilling the will of God in your life, please do not argue with me. Be happy. Just pray for me, that I may be delivered from any error.

But if honestly in your heart you know that you are saved, you know that you are born of God, you know that you are called of God, you know that God has given you some work to do, yet you are terribly conscious of being unclothed, that you do not have the right equipment, that somehow or other you cannot meet the emergencies produced by your calling, you cannot meet the problems that are inherent within the work to which God has called you, then I believe that you may need to take heed to what I say. I want to be quite clear on this matter. It is yours. The anointing is as much a part of your salvation as anything else and in that sense it belongs to you at spiritual birth. The moment Jesus was born of the Holy Spirit He had all the potentiality for the anointing of the Holy Spirit. But there came a point in the ordination of God when Jesus entered His work and not one moment early and not one moment late, God anointed Him with the Holy Spirit and with power. And from that moment for just over three years, Jesus fulfilled a ministry such as this world had never seen or heard.

Offered Up to God

Furthermore, when it came to Gethsemane it was, in my opinion, the Holy Spirit who enabled the Lord Jesus to come right through that anguish which at one point nearly took His physical life when He sweat great drops of blood and angels came to minister to Him. And the writer to the Hebrews says, "By the eternal Spirit He offered Himself up to God without spot or blemish" (Hebrews 9:14). It was by that anointing of the Holy Spirit and of power that in great weakness and humiliation as the apostle Paul said in another way of fallen man: "In much trembling, in much weakness, and in much fear I came amongst you" (1 Corinthians 2:3). In a much deeper and fuller way Jesus, in His weakness and humiliation, was crucified, but by the anointing power of the Holy Spirit He fulfilled the work God gave Him to do. In that moment, the work for which He had come into the world, He finished.

Whatever the theological differences folks may have, the fact remains that the anointing of God is an essential constituent in service. Otherwise, we are like people who know we are saved, know we are born of God, know that God is doing something in us, know that He is producing something in us, conforming us in some way to the image of His Son, know we are called to a ministry, to a work or to a responsibility amongst the people of

God, but know we are always unable to do it. We go around like zombies in the work of God. We honestly do not know what to do, how to cope or what to do. We have to run off to other brothers all the time to ask because we really do not know, we do not have the anointing that comes from God that brings with it the grace and power to know what we should do and the ability to do it. Now do not misunderstand me on this point. It does not mean there is no fellowship, it does not mean there is no counseling. Maybe there will be more fellowship, more counseling than ever before because sometimes the very reason we do not seek counseling is an inferiority complex. We want to stand on our own two feet! It is only when we really have our own experience of the Lord that we can honestly open ourselves up to one another, when we have nothing to fear. So this matter is, in my estimation, of tremendous importance.

General Anointing

I believe there is a distinction to be made between what I would call general anointing and specific anointing. I am very sorry for those meetings where people are belabored, pushed, persuaded, compelled to come forward to have hands laid upon them so that they may receive an anointing. I believe again and again people come before their time and sometimes get an emotional type of experience which very quickly subsides, and then they are left with very real problems. The general side of anointing let me say straightaway is this: in the Lord Jesus every single believer has an anointing and if by faith he abides in it, it operates. I have known even carnal people sometimes to come under the anointing.

Now that may shock you. "Oh!" but you say, "that is impossible!" Oh no, it is not. Who has not been in a real prayer meeting where some person who is about ninety percent flesh suddenly prays under the anointing and we all know it is the Lord. We know they are saved, but what a pain in the neck they are normally because of their carnality and worldly ways. But suddenly, at some point they come forward and they hit the nail right on the head. How come?! Everyone says, "Isn't it strange? There is godly old so-and-so tied up in knots over there and there is so-and-so who is all flesh and suddenly he comes in with prayer that really touches something." Why? Because that person happened to operate under the anointing in that gathering. There is an anointing on the whole body which comes from the Head and goes to every member.

For instance, in I John 2 the apostle is speaking to children, to young men and to fathers, and then he says this: "And ye have an anointing from the Holy One, and ye know all things... And as for you, the anointing which ye received of him abideth in you, and ye need not that any one teach you [that is to what is right or wrong]; but as his anointing teacheth you concerning all things, and is true, and is no lie, and even as it taught you, ye abide in him" (vv. 20, 27).

Now this is for babes as well as young men and fathers spiritually; it is for the whole family. It is a general anointing. There is a general anointing on every gathering of God's people, although very rarely does anybody bother to come under it or seek the Lord concerning the anointing for a gathering. Nevertheless, every time God's people really gather together in the name of the Lord Jesus there is a provision made for that time.

There is an anointing for it so that the will of God can be done in that time, the mind of God might be known in that time and that the meeting may not just be a meeting but may actually lead the people of God further on in the path that God has mapped out for them. It is one of the jobs of leaders. That is why sometimes we should get together before a meeting simply to get into touch with the anointing for that time so that we do not go on in a kind of confusion or in a kind of lethargy or an apathy, but we have put ourselves under the anointing for that time. Now this is general anointing in a sense.

Specific Anointing

But there is such a thing as specific anointing. If God calls you to an apostolic work, He will give you an apostolic anointing. If God calls you to an evangelistic work, He will give you an evangelistic anointing. If God calls you to a teaching ministry, He will give you an anointing for teaching. If God calls you to be a help in the body of Christ He will give you an anointing to be a help. For every single ministry there is an anointing and it is specific. People say to me, "Now is this specific anointing a second experience?" Well here I do not want to be too thunderous on the matter. You see a lot comes into temperament. Some people are not dramatic people. They are not what I call "black and white" people. They very rarely have great emotion; in fact, sometimes they belabor themselves because they never weep, they never cry. They would love to, but they don't. However, God does not condemn them because that is the kind of people they are. Sometimes these people can get an anointing and don't know it.

Even though they may not know it, we all know. I know people who tell me that they do not believe in a second experience, but I knew them before they had it! And the difference in them is between chalk and cheese, night and day, and no one can tell me that something did not happen to them. They say, "Well, of course, I did have dealings with God. I came to an end of myself and this happened." They did not have one of those great earth shattering times where they were taken upside down, turned round, knocked out, laid on the floor and so on, as some others have had, but something happened.

In the history of God's people can anyone tell me of any great servant of the Lord that did not have a specific anointing? I do not know of any. I think of D. L. Moody who lay for a day on the floor. I think of Rubin Torrey who was turned upside down and could not speak for a week. I think of John and Charles Wesley. Charles Wesley got so excited that in the middle of the night he ran out shouting at the top of his voice. Everyone thought he had gone out of his mind. Then he went back and wrote: "Oh for a Thousand Tongues to Sing my Great Redeemer's Praise." John Wesley, well I mean, John Wesley came over to this side, and went up and down these colonies preaching the gospel to the colonials right through these very parts. He knew the gospel and preached it, but he wrote in his journal: "I am seeking to convert the Red Indians, but who will convert me?!" And when he had that strange warming in his heart, which was his new birth, it was not the end; for some time later he had an experience that he called perfect love, but the change in the ministry of John Wesley was distinct.

Austin-Sparks

I remember years ago Mr. Sparks, when I first went to speak with him about my own need and experience. I wondered if perhaps I was mad or the subject of demon influence or something or other. He looked at me and said, "No, you are not mad." He said, "I had something of the same experience and I went to one great evangelical and he told me, 'Go and play golf; get out in the fresh air.'" "I said to him: 'I cannot preach anymore. Everything in me is dead, and I just feel as if I have come to an end of everything.'" He went to another and he told him, "Take a holiday. Go to the Mediterranean. Forget everything for a while and you will be all right." But Mr. Sparks said to me, "I could not accept their advice. I felt there was something I was missing."

Then one day he took his Bible and said to his wife: "You will not see me again until God does something." He went up to his study, shut the door, fell on his knees and said, "God, I am a hypocrite. I cannot go on. Here I am speaking in Keswick-type meetings all over the country, but in my heart I have no real life or power." And he began to read Romans. He came to Romans 6 which he had spoken on again and again. He had talked on the old man that is done away and walking in newness of life, but suddenly, it was if the whole thing came out of the page and hit him. Suddenly he realized that he was crucified with Christ, and it was as if heaven opened and the Holy Spirit fell upon him. And once I said, "Do you believe that there is such a thing as a baptism of the Spirit?" And he said, "Not what a lot of people call a baptism, but there is a baptism of the Holy Spirit and I've had it!" Those people who knew Mr. Sparks before and after that experience all said the same thing; it was like the difference between night and day.

Now I believe that brother Nee had some such experience as well if I am right, but I shall leave that to others to say. The fact of the matter is this: I wonder where you can go in the history of the church where you will not find that if God specifically calls people to a particular job and work He does not specifically anoint them.

Billy Graham

Even in my little experience, I can remember Billy Graham when he first came to England as a young man of twenty-three. Now I was only just saved but I went to hear him. I remember that meeting and the soft blues-type music that was playing in the background and the sob-like appeal that was made. I remember how he nearly leapt over the rail of the pulpit in Westminster Chapel and rolled on the floor wrestling with the lions. It was supposed to be the Christians being eaten by the lions. I had never seen anything like it. I was nearly out of my seat watching him. I never took my eyes off him. It quite saved me because at that time I was almost tempted to go back because it was at the point of my own experience when I was in a great period of darkness and death spiritually. And I thought, "Well if that young man can go to such lengths to try and get somebody saved, there must be something in it."

Then two to three years later Billy Graham came back and I've never forgotten it. By that time I had had my own experience, and I sat there and watched that man. He stood up and took the Bible, whereas before it was all illustration after illustration, wonderful stories and antics, now it was just the Word, the Word, the Word.

And there was no soft playing of music when the appeal was given, but hundreds of people went forward. And I thought, "Whatever has happened to that man?" I heard later that he had had an experience of God. The man was saved, but something happened to him that brought him finally to an end of his own energy and power to somehow produce a ministry and to fulfill a work for God. And God was able to fulfill the work in him that He had given him to do. That is the anointing.

The Significance of Anointing

What is the significance of anointing? Well I don't think that it needs to be said to most of you reading this that it was oil, and oil is the symbol of the Holy Spirit. That is the first thing. The second thing about this oil is that it was poured on, so it is the Holy Spirit coming upon. Now, of course, it is an interesting fact that all through the Old Covenant the Holy Spirit came upon people to do a specific job; the interesting thing was that in the Old Covenant the Holy Spirit was not in them. Now it seems that some people believe that the Holy Spirit is in us, but they do not seem to think that you can have an experience of the Holy Spirit coming upon you! Whatever is wrong with us? We believers are so small in our mind. We can only ever seem to contain one part of the truth at one time. We cannot believe in the sovereignty of God and at the same time believe there is such a thing as human responsibility. We cannot believe in church truth and believe in evangelism. We are either all for deeper, deeper life or all for superficial evangelism. That seems the way many people's minds work. But God has put the two things together. And so it must be. Are we under the New Covenant with the Holy Spirit indwelling in us to throw away the precious truth that the Holy Spirit comes upon us? What kind of service are we going to render? How far are we going to go? You know me (I hope) well enough to know that I am not asking that somehow or other you all become wild, excessive, noisy people rolling around on the floor. Mind you it would do one or two some good! Maybe it would be good for one or two to sort of loosen up just a little—not for all the time but just for a little while. Now it is interesting that sometimes when the Holy Spirit comes upon a person they are knocked out. But I am not asking you to act in some peculiar way, some eccentric way, to act contrary to your own temperament or nature; all I am pleading for is that we know an anointing with the Holy Spirit and with power to do the work God has given us to do.

The United States could be changed if every person in this building today was truly anointed with the Holy Spirit and with power. Think of the potentiality within the ministries that God has given us and within the work to which God has called us. Think of the tremendous scope of the purpose of God into which we believe He has brought us. If we only had that anointing with the Holy Spirit and with power to see God's purpose fulfilled! Then we would be able to war in the place of prayer, to be able to tackle things in the unseen, to be able to come against those works of Satan and see them undone, to be able to see the Word of God communicated in a living vital manner so that the youngest amongst us receives something from God, even if they don't understand everything. It is the oil poured upon the person or upon the thing.

Threefold Meaning of Anointing

There seems to be a threefold meaning of anointing. It seems to me first of all, it seems to mean that whatever is anointed is set aside; it is separated unto the Lord.

The second thing is this: whatever is separated unto the Lord is under divine authority and government. Now the Lord is very, very jealous over this matter. You will remember a prophet who was anointed and was given a word by God to do something and he disobeyed. An older prophet said to him, "Come aside and do not worry about anything that has been said to you. Come aside and stay." And he listened to him. Here is a little exercise of authority. The young prophet should never have listened to the older prophet, and a lion got him and mauled him to death (1 Kings 13:9–24). God is very jealous on the matter of anointing. When a person is anointed, they are separated unto God, and they are not to prostitute what God has given them. They are not to allow it to be adulterated. They are not allowed to water down anything. They are under divine government and authority.

And thirdly, divine grace and wisdom and power is made available to whoever is anointed. In other words, it is not just a question of power, but specific grace, and specific wisdom and specific power is made available to that one anointed to fulfill the job or ministry they have been given to do. Now if that is anointing, I want it. I cannot think of anything more terrible than to be called into the work of God, to be given a vision and understanding of the purpose of God, to be given, as it were, an appreciation of what your ministry is or the work God has given you to do, and then find yourself totally incapable of doing anything.

We know the Lord is the power, but it is the breakthrough of the spiritual sound barrier that I am bothered about, so that though we are weak, we are broken, we are nothing, but He in us is everything. He becomes the power, He becomes the grace, He becomes the wisdom and He becomes the ability. That is anointing.

In spite of what people say sometimes, the people of God have good horse sense. Is it not true? We will go a long way to hear somebody preach who is anointed. People may say they do not believe in anointing, but we can tell in our churches and assemblies who is anointed and who is not. They do not have to stand up on their hind legs for very long before we know exactly where they stand. This is not being critical or judgmental; it is just a fact. One person can sing and all we are left with is their singing, and another person can sing and the Lord ministers to us. One person can play the piano and all we are left with is their technique; another person can play the piano and it is as if the Lord stirs our spirit. One person can preach and we hear words and thoughts and sometimes wonderful thoughts, but it does not do anything to us; another person preaches and it as if a sword goes into our being. It is the difference between the un-anointed and the anointed.

The Place of Temperament in Anointing

Isaiah and Ezekiel

What about the place of temperament in anointing? One of the most interesting things is this and I find it one of the glories of the Word of God, that everyone who is used of God is no automaton.

Isaiah remains Isaiah. His royal blood, his sophisticated background, his education, his very temperament comes right through that infallible, authoritative, inspired Word of God. Isaiah remains Isaiah and Ezekiel remains Ezekiel. I always felt that Ezekiel was a mathematician. I am dying to see him for this reason. I think I am right. A person's temperament never changes, and I think we shall find that Ezekiel was of a more scientific bent of mind; for example, being able to describe a vision such as he saw. Certainly God knew that. I can imagine God saying, "It is no good giving Isaiah a vision like I am going to give Ezekiel because the man could not describe it." There were wheels within wheels, going straight this way and that way and so on. Isaiah just could not do it, but Ezekiel could understand.

You see, God knows just what He is doing with His servants. Before they are even born He is forming them in their mother's womb. He knows their grandparents and their great grandparents and their great-great grandparents and their great-great-great grandparents. Their genetic history is all out before God marvelously foreordained. No servant of the Lord is a mistake, even though sometimes we think it. We who are the recipients of their work and ministry sometimes feel, "Oh dear, so-and-so." But God has made no mistake. When He has a special thing to convey, He creates a special vessel. When He has a special aspect of truth or a special truth to communicate, He creates a vessel that is peculiarly suited for that ministry. Ezekiel is Ezekiel; you will not confound him with Isaiah because the way he puts things is not the same.

Jeremiah

And what about Jeremiah? Oh! Jeremiah is the psychologist's paradise. He cannot go very far before he is talking about himself. He starts out saying, and it is all in the Book: "Oh Lord! I wish you had not put me here! I have said many times I will never say another thing." And then he says, "Then the fire burnt in my bones and I could not do anything else and here I am speaking again (see Jeremiah 20:7–9). Jeremiah is on every page of his prophesies; he cannot help it. It is not that he is self-centered; he is a different type of man. You do not confound Jeremiah with Isaiah or Ezekiel, do you? They are quite different.

Paul and James

And if you think that is only Old Testament, come over to the New Testament and you will never confound Paul with James. Paul says things that James could not say and James says things that Paul could not say; they would choke in his throat. James says, "Do you see that you are not justified by faith alone but by works also?" (James 2:24). We know very well he is saying the same thing as Paul. He did not mean that you are justified by works of your own, but he meant by a working faith, a faith that operates, a faith that is concretely expressed in action. But Paul could not have said it the same way. Paul labored on this: "You see! You are saved by faith alone and not by works!" (Romans 3:28). And here is James saying, "You see! You are saved by faith and works." "Now how come?" Some people will say, "Well, of course, the Bible is not inspired." No, that is not so at all. The glory of it is this: James is the kind of man that God says something that is through James and the stamp of James' temperament and personality remains on his contribution rightly. It is not a mistake. It is not as if God says, "Well, I wish I could get James out of this, but since I cannot, I will just have to take him in with it." No, it is by ordination. It is by foreordination. That man James could only say the things he could say and see the things which he saw because of who he was and what he was and the type of person he was. When the anointing comes upon him, it modifies his excesses. It balances what could be extremes. But he remains essentially the temperament he was. And so it is with Paul.

John

Let us consider John. Does anybody write like the apostle John in the New Testament? I think even the youngest believer who knows their Bible or who has just started reading their Bible would be able to tell the style of John. John has a very black and white style, does he not? He is not at all like Paul. So you have three quite different men and yet all inspired, and equally valuable. It is not as if we can say, "Now Paul is our man, John comes next and James—well, James was bound."

Peter

And then you've even got Peter, and in one of his letters he actually says, "Our beloved brother Paul who writes things very hard to be understood" (II Peter 3:15–16). And it is all in the book! Do you not think that is amazing? These men are anointed. Here is the anointed Peter writing a letter and he actually says that Paul says things which are hard to be understood. I am sure that if he had realized thousands of believers all down through the centuries were going to study the words, Peter would have felt self-conscious: "I will take that out!" I have often thought that about Paul when he wrote, "Oh!" he said, "you have pushed me, you Corinthians. You have pushed me over and now I have to say this and this" (ii Corinthians 12:11–19). And then he says, "When I wrote that letter to you, I was overcome with grief and sorrow. I felt I should not have written it. But now I have got news about you and I am so glad I wrote it" (ii Corinthians 2:4; 7:8). Well I am glad he wrote it because it was the I Corinthian letter, but there was the apostle having a bad time over what was inspired and infallible scripture. Is it not interesting how God deals with His servants even when they are anointed? He allows them to go through their bad times and even allows them to have doubts. Some of us when we minister most powerfully in the Lord are least conscious of it and go away to have a bad time about it and think, "Oh that was dreadful. Dear Lord, deliver me from that kind of thing again. I will not do it again." Then we find out that people got saved, some got blessed, and others met the Lord and all the rest of it. Is it not amazing? I have found that when I thought the Lord has been with me, generally speaking, He was not. And when I thought the Lord was not with me, I found out afterwards He was! It is strange, this matter of anointing.

You see the idea that some people have got is a kind of pagan spiritualist idea that when the Holy Spirit comes upon you and you become like a tank. You are sort of immovable; you can bulldoze anything! You are absolutely strong and know that God is with you! You know exactly what you have got to say and you say it. It is this mediumistic type of inspiration and anointing where an evil spirit comes upon a medium and possesses them and manipulates them. They do not even know what they are doing, but they know they have got to say this and this and this. This is not Biblical or spiritual anointing or inspiration at all. At all times the spirit of the prophet is under the control of the prophet (I Corinthians 14:32). The prophet may not know exactly the full extent of what he is saying, but he does know what he is saying.

A Supernatural Work

This matter of anointing is therefore very, very important. And if we can get this matter of temperament clear, we shall understand the dear apostle Paul when he says, "I was with you in much fear ..." We would say, "Paul, you need deliverance." "Much fear, much weakness." "Oh my! You need a healing ministry." "And much trembling" (see I Corinthians 2:3). "Trembling? Perhaps he has high blood pressure. Why was he trembling? He needs to know the Holy Spirit." And it is an interesting fact that Paul says in one of his letters that "some of you say that when I am present, I am very weak" (II Corinthians 10:1). So the impression sometimes given was one that people could easily say, "He is walking in the flesh" (v. 2b). But then he said, "My preaching was not in persuasive words of man's wisdom but in demonstration of the Spirit and of power: that your faith might not stand in the wisdom of men, but in the power of God" (I Corinthians 2:4). Now every time (listen to me carefully) a servant of the Lord ministers without the anointing the people end up trusting in man's wisdom. They trust in that man's ability. They trust in that man's teaching or whatever else, but when it is under the anointing, they end up trusting in the power of God. Anointing enables a man or a woman to do a supernatural work. It is not like lecturing in a university or a college, but it is actually communicating the Lord Jesus to people so that they receive Him; they receive more of Him.

Obtaining the Anointing

I want to say something about the obtaining of this anointing. May I say first of all that all the work done for any child of God to be anointed has been finished by the Lord Jesus. There is nothing you have to do. It is not given on the basis of your merit or your goodness or your zeal; it is given on the ground that Jesus has perfectly won your salvation. That is the first thing.

The second thing I want to say is this: We learn a lot from the anointing of the Lord Jesus. In Matthew 3 we read the account of His baptism: "Then cometh Jesus from Galilee to the Jordan unto John, to be baptized of him. But John would have hindered him, saying, I have need to be baptized of thee, and comest thou to me? But Jesus answering, said unto him, Suffer it now: for thus it becometh us to fulfil all righteousness. Then he suffereth him. And Jesus, when he was baptized, went up straightway from the water: and lo, the heavens were opened unto him, and he saw the Spirit of God descending as a dove, and coming upon him; and lo, a voice out of the heavens, saying, This is my beloved Son, in whom I am well pleased" (vv. 13–17).

What did He do? He obeyed His father explicitly. That is the first thing. Secondly, He committed Himself to the will of God at that time whatever the price. And thirdly, He laid down His life as far as self-centeredness, self-assertion or self-fulfillment was concerned. Now that is the baptism of Jesus. That is why He went into the waters of Jordan. They represented for Him not the need for His sins to be washed away, but they spoke symbolically of the death of the cross. And three years before He came to the cross He said, "Father, I commit myself to the work of the cross," and laid down His life. Then the Holy Spirit came upon Him to enable Him to fulfill the work which God was giving Him to do not only in the three years of His ministry, but in that final supreme work of atonement.

Now if you and I would know such an anointing, I will make these comments. First of all, God has a timing for you. It may be tonight, it may be a year, it may be five years away, but God has a timing. Do not give up! Do not give up! Seek and seek and seek. Be honest, be pure in heart, and never give up. If it is of any encouragement to any of you, the Bible says, "Blessed are the pure in heart for they shall see God" (Matthew 5:8). Jacob was one of the biggest twisters in the world, but he was pure in heart, (think that one out) because he saw God. He said, "I have seen the face of God and I have lived" (Genesis 32:30). With all the other manipulations of his mind and everything else, in his heart there was a sincerity. As far as God was concerned there was a purity in the man's heart. He was honest with God in his heart of hearts. There is a time. Do not give up, go on. Some of these men like Wesley and others sought the Lord for years. I know people who have sought the Lord for months solidly, but I have never known anyone who has sought the Lord for an anointing who has not in the end been anointed.

Secondly, you must be called of God. God never anoints you for a job if He did not call you to it. So if you are in a job of ministry or responsibility that you should not be in, God will never anoint you because unless He has called you to it, He does not anoint you for such a job. You must be called of God.

Thirdly, you must be ready for His will whatever the cost. Maybe God will send you to Nepal, to New Guinea, to Europe or Alaska; I do not know. Maybe God will keep you in some humdrum job locally. I do not know, but you must be ready for the will of God whatever the cost.

Fourthly, you must be thirsty for all that He has provided. God will never ever anoint a man or a woman who would devalue the anointing. You must be thirsty for everything God has provided.

Fifthly, you must be at an end of your own resources. Maybe that is why God will keep you waiting for a while. He has to burn up all that strength of will and all those resources of your own. You must be at an end of your own resources.

And lastly, you must lay down your life. God will never anoint anybody who does not lay down their life. The other kind of thing is human charisma, but it is not anointing. Once you have said, "Not I but Christ," once you are ready to lay down your life totally for Him, He will anoint you. You cannot do it of yourself, you can only be willing to do it, ready to do it. He will take you that way, do not worry. There has to come in your life, as in Jesus, a committal to those waters. A readiness just to go down and say, "Lord, I am not sure all that it is going to cost, but I lay down my life in principle this night, this day. Hear me, Lord, and set your seal upon it." May God help us all in this because there could be no more important matter in leadership or in any holding of responsibility in the work of God than this matter of anointing.

9.
The Character of Spiritual Leadership

Before I go on, I would like to clarify two points in answer to questions about the anointing for service.

Quite a number of people have asked whether the anointing is a kind of static thing, whether you can lose the power of it, or whether it is to increase in power. In my estimation the anointing is a very real and distinct coming upon a servant of the Lord. Even if that one is not overly conscious (and most are conscious that something has happened and they know it is the Lord), everyone around is conscious that something has happened to them. However, just because a person is anointed with the Spirit does not mean that through the years they will not compromise that anointing or in some way contradict it and therefore lose the power and operation of that anointing.

The second thing is that an anointing, while it may be an initial experience, can grow in depth and power. It is linked with the character of spiritual leadership. In other words, an anointing can come upon someone who is quite young and does not have a great spiritual capacity. They can operate up to their spiritual capacity and the Lord can convey and communicate something through them. But the greater the capacity, the deeper the walk with the Lord, the greater the understanding of the Lord, and the greater the expansion of that person's spirit in the Lord, the more the anointing can operate and the more the Lord can convey Himself through that vessel.

Another question that was asked is this: Once an anointing is given, is it ever taken away? Of course, I suppose people must think of King Saul who was anointed but whose anointing was taken away. I think this is a rather difficult question to answer and the only way I can answer it at present is to turn you to Romans 11:29: "The gifts and the calling of God are irrevocable." Now if the gifts and the calling of God are irrevocable, one would have thought that the anointing was also. I think we must see it in the light of what I have just said, that if a person compromises that anointing, contradicts it continually, there could come a point where it ceases to operate although it is still there. It is, as it were, paralyzed.

The Worker is More Important than the Work

We want to consider this matter of the character of spiritual leadership, and in my estimation, whilst the exercise of authority and being under authority in order to exercise authority is vital, and whilst the matter of the anointing is necessary and essential, this matter of character is all important. We have all suffered from leadership which has very little spiritual character. Spiritual character, spiritual experience, and spiritual history are vital to leadership in the sight of God.

First of all, the worker is more important to God than even His work. Let me repeat that: The worker is more important to God than even his work. God has in view an eternal vocation. He is not impervious to all the needs of His people down here, but there are times when because He has a candidate for a high position in His eternal administration, He will take that worker, that servant, and put him or her on one side for a while or allow the inexplicable to come in. Why is this so? Because the worker is far more important to God in the ultimate than even his work. The work is very important to God, but if it is a question of work with the worker having a poor character, God would prefer to take the worker out of the work and do something about the character. So in this matter of spiritual character we must always remember that the worker is more important to God than even His work.

He took Amy Carmichael, crippled her, put her on a bed for twenty-six years, and did a very real and deep work in her which created and produced a ministry to those who suffer inexplicably. I do not know any other ministry that comes near to it. I never knew her personally, but there were those, some of whom were my friends and have since passed on to be with the Lord, who knew Amy Carmichael very well indeed as a personal friend. They said that when she was young she was like the wind. She was always active, rushing here, rushing there, and in fact one of the most characteristic things concerning her was to see her on a bicycle with her hair flying behind her cycling absolutely full speed across the compound. Everything was done at a military pace. Everything had to be done swiftly. She was a very energetic person. God took her in the most incredible and sovereign way and put her on her back and then began her worldwide ministry to the people of God through her writings. What God did in her is a good example of the worker being more important to God than the work she was doing. In the end He had something higher in mind, not only for time but for eternity.

The Work Done in the Worker

We will find this in II Corinthians 1: "Blessed be the God and Father of our Lord Jesus Christ, the Father of mercies and God of all comfort; who comforteth us in all our affliction, that we may be able to comfort them that are in any affliction, through the comfort wherewith we ourselves are comforted of God" (vv. 3–4).

Do you see the principle? It is not just passing on pious phrases or spiritual truths, but something has happened inside that servant of the Lord that enables them to speak to the problem in somebody else. "Deep calls unto deep" (Psalm 42:7).

"For as the sufferings of Christ abound unto us, even so our comfort also aboundeth through Christ. But whether we are afflicted, it is for your comfort and salvation; or whether we are comforted, it is for your comfort, which worketh in the patient enduring of the same sufferings which we also suffer: and our hope for you is steadfast; knowing that, as ye are partakers of the sufferings, so also are ye of the comfort. For we would not have you ignorant, brethren, concerning our affliction which befell us in Asia, that we were weighed down exceedingly, beyond our power, insomuch that we despaired even of life: yea, we ourselves have had the sentence of death within ourselves, that we should not trust in ourselves, but in God who raiseth the dead:

who delivered us out of so great a death, and will deliver: on whom we have set our hope that he will also still deliver us" (II Corinthians 1:5–10).

Here is a work being done in the workers, Paul and his little party. They are not just speaking out of their head knowledge; they are speaking not only out of an understanding and illumination of the Word of God by the Holy Spirit, but they are speaking out of their own experience. They are themselves having to prove the Lord.

Some people will immediately say to me: "Are you saying that we who have a ministry of the Word should never ever speak about anything which is not our experience?" Of course that is nonsense. Supposing we were to confine ourselves to only what we have personally experienced? It is going to cut down ministry very much and our horizons would not be too wide. We could not describe the kingdom to come; we could not describe the things that are going to be, because we have not yet had our own experience of those things. Think of what has been given to us in this Book; the writers did not always have a full experience of everything. But what I am trying to say is that sometimes we who are leaders convey and communicate truth that is not yet ours and God goes about making it ours. There are other times when we already have the experience and out of that experience comes the ministry. The principle for God is that the worker is, in the end, more important than even the work. In fact, I think we could go so far as to say that the worker is the work of God. In the final analysis, what God does in His servants is the way He is going to work through them in others. So this matter is a very important one.

Kept Humble

In II Corinthians 12 the apostle Paul tells us that he was caught up to the third heaven and he heard things that it was not even lawful for a man to utter. Then he says, "And by reason of the exceeding greatness of the revelations, that I should not be exalted overmuch, there was given to me a thorn in the flesh, a messenger of Satan to buffet me, that I should not be exalted overmuch. Concerning this thing I besought the Lord thrice, that it might depart from me. And he hath said unto me, My grace is sufficient for thee: for my power is made perfect in weakness. Most gladly therefore will I rather glory in my weaknesses, that the power of Christ may rest upon me [or tabernacle upon me]. Wherefore I take pleasure in weaknesses, in injuries, in necessities, in persecutions, in distresses, for Christ's sake: for when I am weak, then am I strong" (vv. 7–10).

Here again we see the worker is more important to God than the work. If the work and not the worker were so important to God, He could give these tremendous revelations to a man but would not bother about keeping the man humble and broken in order to see that the man is totally dependent upon Him. But because this vessel is so precious to God and because in the final analysis that servant is the work of God, He will go to the extent of even giving him a messenger from Satan. Conybeare translated this rather dramatically but very vividly and I think in a memorable way, as "the agony of impalement." That is a little bit more than a thorn in the flesh. Of course, if you have a thorn in your foot or in your finger, after a while it is not long before your whole hand, arm or leg throbs. You do feel that little thing, but think of it as the agony of impalement and maybe that will bring you nearer to an understanding of this messenger of Satan. It was something which crucified the apostle. It was something that impaled him on a stake so that he could not move. He was so weak he just had to depend upon God.

Now here again we see that the worker is more important than the work he does. I hope this is not frightening to death those of you who are either beginning to serve the Lord or who in fact will come into the work of God. But here we have a very important principle, that what you have seen so far with the eye of your heart, that which is not yet yours in true experience and history, God will go about making it your experience and history. If you are a candidate for the throne, if you are a candidate for the bride, I can tell you that God will be very, very careful to make what you see your own experience and history.

Paul – A Drink Offering

There is one more scripture in this connection which is very interesting. In II Timothy 4: 6, we have the apostle putting into the most beautiful words his sense of going: "For I am already being offered." I suggest that if this was not first in the Word of God, no one would ever think of their death, their decapitation, as a being offered. But here we see the worker is more important than the work. The apostle sees his last months or whatever they were as a being offered, a being poured out as a drink offering. If you look back at Philippians, written probably from his imprisonment in Rome (although some think it was written in Israel in Caesarea in his earlier imprisonment whilst waiting to go to Rome), he writes: "Yea, and if I am offered upon the sacrifice and service of your faith, I joy, and rejoice with you all" (2:17). It is the same word again: "If I am being poured out as a drink offering." He was himself something. God was doing something in him and, as it were, pouring him out. That is the first thing I would like to say about the character of true leadership: the worker is far more important to God than even the work which has been given him to do.

Do not think any of us are indispensable. The work could probably be done by a hundred others. I do not personally believe that anyone can do a job. God specially forms and produces people for the work to be done. But with any particular work that He has to do, God is able to produce a number of people who could do it; therefore none of us are indispensable. But what He does in a worker is unique. No two servants of the Lord are absolutely alike; they are not peas in a pod. They are all different because of the way God deals with them.

Hearing and Seeing the Lord

The second thing I would like to say about the character of true leadership is that it is a matter of seeing and hearing. Above everything else, a true leader must see the Lord. What hope is there for the flock if the leaders do not see the Lord? I do not mean, as you all must understand, physical visions of the Lord, although personally I am not against anyone having an actual vision of the Lord. The more the better in these days of stress and strain as long as they do not lead us astray or make us big-headed. But I am talking about that vision which is an understanding with the heart, with the spirit. In other words, "the eyes of our heart," as the apostle Paul said in Ephesians 1: "That the God of our

Lord Jesus Christ, the Father of glory, may give unto you a spirit of wisdom and revelation in the knowledge of him; having the eyes of your heart enlightened, that ye may know what is the hope of his calling" (vv. 17–18).

This matter of seeing is tremendously important. Jesus once spoke of blind leaders leading the blind and both falling into the ditch (Matthew 15:14). Church history is filled with the evidence of blind leaders leading the blind people of God and both falling into the ditch. The character of spiritual leadership is determined by seeing and hearing the Lord. There could be no matter more important than this.

Leaders Must Be Examples

A third thing I would like to say about the character of true leadership is that we must be examples. All these things come one out of the other. 1 Timothy 4:12 says, "Let no man despise thy youth; but be thou an ensample to them that believe, in word, in manner of life, in love, in faith, in purity."

We have this again in 1 Peter 5:3 "Neither as lording it over the charge allotted to you, but making yourselves examples to the flock."

It is not officialdom, nor the holding merely of status, but genuine examples. It is an interesting thing that when the apostle wrote the letters to Timothy and Titus and mentioned elders and deacons, all the qualifications he gave for them were to do with character—how they govern their children, how their relationship of husband to wife was going on, even what people said of them outside who were not saved. Now that is a very interesting thing, is it not? What do the unsaved people say about this believer? It is not anything to do with officialdom, with status, with title, as if you shove a person into an office and then they become an elder. You sort of push them into a place and give them a title and immediately they become the function that we put them into. No, no, it is not that. There has got to be character. It is an organic thing. And this matter of example I think is very, very important indeed. We need to be examples in everything.

Now we all fall short on this, do we not? What servant of the Lord does not fall short in this matter? If we really want to pick to pieces any servant of the Lord, we can, I do not care who it is. I am quite sure that if we had the apostles here, including the apostle Paul, it would be possible to pick him to pieces if we wanted to. When you read some of the letters and look at some of the things that he said, we do not usually dwell on that. It is quite clear that those who knew the apostle Paul could pick him to pieces if they wanted to. The fact that the churches in Asia turned away I do not think was only a matter to do with the vision that God had given to him. I reckon that the Judaizers had gotten to work and probably said, "You see, the man is this, the man is that; the man does this." Nearly always there is some legitimate ground for picking to pieces a servant of the Lord.

I remember something Miss Fischbacher said to me years ago when I was asking about brother Nee and at the time it quite shocked me, but since then has been quite a blessing. She said, "The higher a man goes, the deeper he can fall, and the greater the man is, the bigger his faults and the more they are seen." I think it is true. I remember a statement by a Muslim holy man from the sixteenth-seventeenth century which always amused me.

He said, "Thank you, God, that the people do not know me as You do." In one sense, it is very true. If we really knew one another we could pick them to pieces. But having said that, in all our frailty, in all our weakness, in all our tendency to collapse, we need to be examples above everything else. And it is interesting how the apostle says to Timothy to be an example—"in word, in manner of life, in love, in faith, in purity." We need to take heed to that.

Pioneering

Now I want to underline another word which may help us. I think the character of true leadership is pioneering. Of course it is a matter of example but the idea of pioneering perhaps focuses the thought better. What is a leader? A leader is someone who leads. It is as simple as that. He is a pioneer, therefore he is out in front. He is not at the back in some comfortable little office while everyone else is like cannon fodder on the war front, but he is there in front. One of the nice things, although I always feel it is very sad that in the wars we have had the officers in the Israeli army lead the men from the top general right the way down. That is why in every war the relative casualty figure is higher amongst the officers than the men. Now this is not so with the armies in Britain or Western Europe. The officers normally stay in the background and the men go out in front. But the old way was to lead the men into war, and if an officer could not lead them right in the forefront he was not worth his salt. And so it certainly seems to me it should be amongst the people of God. Leaders are not those who never come to a prayer meeting or never spend the night in prayer or never know anything about real sacrifice and never know what it is to really suffer in one way or another, but they are to be pioneers in all these things, right in the forefront of the battle.

In the letter to the Hebrews 13:7 it implies this: "Remember them that had the rule over you, men that spake unto you the Word of God; and considering the issue of their life, imitate their faith." That is a wonderful thing that could be said about any leader, is it not?—"imitate their faith." They were pioneers and we can imitate them in this matter.

Genuine Care and Love

Another thing about the character of true leadership is that there should be a genuine care and love for the people of God. I must tell you that I find again and again the greatest disappointment in the work of God is to find leaders who are not really caring for the flock of God. It becomes apparent that they are there because they think they have a ministry or they think that they have a position. They want to be something in the house of God, they want to be something in the body of Christ. They do not have a genuine love and care for the people of God. Now I realize that everybody cannot give their time totally to visiting or going to prisons or whatever else is involved in visiting. But there is a vast difference between those who are so full of genuine love for the people of God that it pains them and hurts them when things go wrong. In other words, it is this genuine love and care that lies behind the visiting. It is not a duty; it is because they want to tend the lambs, they want to shepherd the sheep. They really want to do it because they care for the flock of God and they care for the building up of the house of God.

In this matter of prayer, leaders should not have to drag themselves along to a time of prayer or when they get together they should not have to say, "Well, we ought to have a time of prayer," but rather there is such a pain inside over some of the problems amongst the people of God that they are driven before God's face in prayer. It is the love that results in prayer warfare. It is not that we say, "Now we must pray because prayer is an important duty." But rather, it is because we have such a care and love for the people of God that when we see the problems, when we see the needs, when we see the onslaught of the enemy or when we see some new phase into which we are moving, we are driven before God to cover it in prayer. This is genuine care and love. As is found in John 21: "Tend My lambs, shepherd My sheep, tend My sheep. Do you love Me? Tend My lambs, shepherd My sheep." This is a genuine love and care for the people of God.

A Teachable Spirit

And then I would like to say something about a teachable spirit. When we become something, then we suddenly have an unteachable spirit. I do not know whether it is an inferiority complex or what it is that somehow makes us feel that we cannot be open to correction or open to balance or whatever else. But one of the most important things about true leadership is that it will learn from anyone and anything. You can learn from the humblest old sister in the assembly. You can learn from the youngest newborn babe in the assembly. You can even learn from those who have a critical spirit. A teachable spirit is beyond price because it means a leader or a servant of the Lord is always going on; they are not static; they have not arrived. Some people have the idea of leadership being like a tape recorder. You press a button and you take in everything for a while and record it. Then at a certain point when you become yourself a teacher or a preacher or a leader or a "servant of the Lord" you then press the button and it all comes out.

Now we do have to take in but there does not come a time when we stop taking in. And there are some people who are servants of the Lord who only think that the only way they can take in is directly from heaven. They have a kind of hotline to heaven. They cannot learn a thing from anybody other than the Lord Himself and some choice servants of the Lord that they feel are elite. But in actual fact the servant of the Lord can learn from Satan. You can learn more from what Satan does and how he does it and how God uses him and overrules him to blessing than many other ways. You can learn from anything. So the person in your assembly who is so difficult may be your greatest teacher in the hand of God. And the other colleague that sort of rubs you up the wrong way all the time may be in fact your greatest instructor in the Lord.

I do not know about any scripture for this other than of course meekness, but there is a very interesting phrase in II Timothy 2:24–25: "And the Lord's servant must not strive, but be gentle towards all, apt to teach, forbearing, in meekness correcting them that oppose themselves; if peradventure God may give them repentance unto the knowledge of the truth."

The Producing of Such Character

Now I would like to say something about the producing of such character. If this is the kind of character that leadership should have, how is it produced? It is produced in two ways and only two ways. Upon that I think we can be quite dogmatic. It is produced through the work of the cross, no less, no more. There is no other way for real character to be produced in a servant of the Lord other than their going the way of the cross.

What do we mean by "the way of the cross"? There has to be a dealing with self all the way through. There has to be a dealing with difficult people all the way through. It is learning how to deal with yourself and the problems that you find within your self-life. It is learning how to deal with difficult people that only through the way of the cross can you learn this. It is learning how to deal with complex and, humanly speaking, insoluble problems that God will allow to come into your path. Only through the way of the cross will you learn. Sometimes when we have a problem, our way is to attack it full on, especially if it happens to have personalities in it that are perhaps against you. So you want to just sort of go at it fully. This is not the way. God says humble yourselves under the mighty hand of God that He may exalt you in due time (1 Peter 5:6). That which exalts itself shall be abased and that which humbles itself shall be exalted (Matthew 23:12). It is an infallible law with God.

Now sometimes we deal with situations in the work of God as if those situations are merely flesh and blood. But if we go the way of the cross and know what it is to be crucified with Christ and know what it is to live by the faith of the Son of God who loved you and gave Himself for you, then you will find that sometimes the way you have to deal with a situation is to do nothing. And it seems to be the most stupid and silly thing in the whole world to sit there and do nothing, but that is exactly the way God will deal with a situation sometimes.

Other times you must fully accept the kind of criticism that is leveled against you or whatever it might be and learn from it and even adjust to it. And there are other times when the way of the cross means you stand up and say something. Now only God the Holy Spirit can show us which applies in any given situation. But this is what I am trying to say: the apostle Paul said by the Spirit of God, "I have been crucified with Christ; and it is no longer I that live, but Christ liveth in me: and that life which I now live in the flesh I live in faith, the faith which is in the Son of God, who loved me, and gave himself up for me" (Galatians 2:20).

Jesus said: "Except a grain of wheat fall into the earth and die, it abideth by itself alone; but if it die, it beareth much fruit...If any man serve me, let him follow me; and where I am, there shall also my servant be" (John 12:24, 26a).

"And where I am"—I do not think He meant that "where I am one day my servant will be." Of course, that is true, but I believe that Jesus actually meant if you will really follow Him He will bring you to the place where you reign with Him now in that situation because you have learned to fall into the ground and die! The problem is not living; the problem is dying. People tell us again and again, "Oh, the problem is living! I find it so hard to overcome! I find it so hard to survive, I find it so hard to get above this thing, I find it so hard to maintain spiritual life in these circumstances." That is not the problem! The devil is getting you to look at the wrong aspect. That is not the problem! The problem is how to die. If you learn how to die God will take care of how you live. When you go down, God takes you up. When you are broken, God will make you whole. When you suffer God will glorify you, when you know what it is to fall into the ground and die God brings a harvest. It is God's business, not yours. This is the principle of the cross. We have deep within us a self-preservation instinct; therefore you cannot go this way but by the faith of the Son of God who loved you and gave Himself for you. There is something inside that says, "Don't! Don't! If you lay down, your reputation will be destroyed by these people. If you allow this thing to go on, your ministry will be finished!" or whatever. But the word of faith says: "Die and God will take care of your name and your ministry and your work." It is a way of faith.

This is not idealistic; it is intensely realistic and practical. Your problem as servants of the Lord, as leaders, is to learn how to die. And you cannot expect all the other children of God in the flock allotted to your charge to fall into the ground and die if they do not see you falling into the ground and dying. We can all preach an ethic. We can all preach a truth, but when it comes to it, we may deny it in our practice. So this matter of the cross is all important because it is the way God produces character.

Think what happens when you have come to the place where it seems to be the end of everything and you let go. You go down and it seems as if all hell is let loose. Do not think for a moment God raises us up as we like to think—we go down and before our head has gone under the water He has taken us up and lifted us high! No. I was going to say God does it solemnly, but sometimes I think He does it with great humor. He deliberately waits until we have gone down three times. Normally we are nearly drowned before at the last moment and at our wits end the Lord comes. And sometimes I must tell you it is beyond our wits end when literally we have had the sentence of death within ourselves so much that we feel we are finished. Then when everything seems as if God has left the body three days, you know it is buried, it is finished, then He steps in and does something. When God touches a situation with a servant of the Lord who has fallen into the ground and died, He always does it completely. And when you come out and see what God has done, those who were against you disappear. The enemy has simply fled. It is gone and then you have your own experience of the Lord, and there is more spiritual character.

What is this spiritual character? It is the way of faith because you have learned that when you trust God, you will not be put to shame. You trusted the Lord when every voice in you said, "Don't be silly, don't be silly; you will never come out of this if you do not do something." But when you died to it, God finally acted and you came through. There is something deep within like a solid rock, and you know that God is utterly dependable.

The trouble with so many servants of the Lord is that their hands are upon the work of the Lord in a vise-like grip. Many servants of the Lord kill the work of the Lord because of their grip on it, and that is why so often God has to take us this way of the cross. It is the producing of character.

Through the Holy Spirit
The second thing about the producing of such character is through the Holy Spirit. If there is any servant of the Lord who is afraid

of the work of the Holy Spirit he or she will not be enabled to serve God. Anyone who is afraid of some aspect of the Person and work of the Holy Spirit will never be able to serve God acceptably because you cannot fall into the ground and die except by the Holy Spirit. You cannot put to death the deeds of the body except by the Holy Spirit. We can make the teaching of the cross, the way of the cross, an abject, heavy, dull bondage and people are all sort of going round like shadows. It is not the real thing at all. Jesus does not bind us; He frees us. The way of the cross is not to put us into bondage; it is to bring us out into liberty. It is to deliver us from the old man; it is to deliver us from the old creation; it is to deliver us from the world and its ways.

So the Spirit of God, His Person and work, are all important in the producing of this kind of character, and I am speaking not only of His indwelling but of His imparting. I am not only speaking of His fruit; I am speaking of His gifts. Do not despise anything. People sometimes come to me after years and years and years of despising the gift of tongues and then they say, "I sought the Lord for a year about the Spirit and He has not given it to me." Of course not. You do not think you can trample some gift under foot and say, "It is kindergarten! It is just childhood! It is nothing! I do not want it! I want the Lord! I do not want it!" And then you expect the moment you see something else God will just shower it upon you like that. Not so! God is very careful. I hope you do not misunderstand me, but He never casts pearl before swine, lest they trample it under foot.

We have to have a right attitude to God. We have to have a right attitude to the gifts of God. We have to be pure in heart. This does not mean that we do not have a twistedness up here in the mind, but in our spirit there is an essential purity. We want the Lord, we are honest with the Lord, and we are prepared to go the whole way with the Lord. This matter of the Holy Spirit, His Person and His work, is vital. There can be no character produced in any servant of the Lord unless the Holy Spirit is the agent. So may I underline this.

Injunctions Given to Leaders

Take Heed to Yourselves

There are, as far as I can see, there may be more, but as far as I can see there are three injunctions, almost warnings, given to leaders. Of course I am not thinking of the one that says, "Be not many teachers, brethren, for they have a harder time of it in the end" (James 3:1). But I was thinking of this: "Take heed to yourself." This is in Acts 20:28 and it says this: "Take heed unto yourselves, and to all the flock, in which the Holy Spirit hath made you bishops." Here are men who are elders, who are bishops, who are overseers and the Lord is saying to them, "Take heed to yourselves." It seems a strange way of putting it. You would have thought He would have said, "Take heed to the flock which I have given you and over which I have made you overseers, and then just remember yourselves." But the apostle says by the Spirit of God, "Take heed to yourselves."

In 1 Timothy 4:16 we read this: "Take heed to thyself and to thy teaching," the apostle says to Timothy. And in 1 Corinthians 10:11 the apostle says, "Let him that thinketh he standeth take heed lest he fall." Galatians 6:1 says, "When you restore a person remember yourself lest you also be tempted." There is no servant of the

Lord who cannot go off the rails. If we take the Word of God as it stands, it seems that nearly every great servant of the Lord in the Bible, certainly in the Old Covenant went off the rails at the end. Having been used of God in the most tremendous way, we find again and again that they did the most terrible things. Noah got drunk, Abraham lied and did other things. Everywhere we find the same, and we are not any different. "Take heed to yourselves."

Guard What Has Been Committed to You

The second thing is this: Guard what has been committed to you. Do not just think it is there and it cannot be taken from you, that you cannot be robbed of it; guard what has been given to you. II Timothy 1:14 says, "That good thing which was committed unto thee guard through the Holy Spirit which dwelleth in us." Or again in I Timothy 6:20: "O Timothy, guard that which is committed unto thee, turning away from the profane babblings and oppositions of the knowledge which is falsely so called." Guard that which has been committed to you. Has God given you something? Has God deposited something in you? Is there something of Himself which He has given to you to contribute to the people of God? Guard it. Guard that vision which He has given you. Guard that understanding that He has so mercifully granted to you. Guard that experience which He has given that it does not evaporate or drain away or become a cause of pride. Guard that which the Lord has given to you by the Holy Spirit.

Stir Up the Gift Which is in You

And thirdly, in II Timothy 1:6 it says, " For which cause I put thee in remembrance that thou stir up the gift of God, which is in thee through the laying on of my hands." What an interesting word this is, "stir into life." It is the thought of stirring embers in a fire—stir it, poke it, give it a good poke, get the ash out. As some servants of the Lord get older there is a lot of ash. It is not that there was not a tremendous amount that God has done in our history and experience, but as we get older, there is ash and more ash and more ash, and if you know anything about a living fire, it is simply this: ash deadens it. You have to rake all the ash out and stir the embers and they will burst back into flame. It is not that the gift which God has given you is slowly disappearing or evaporating or fading; it is there but it has been clogged by dead ash. Get rid of it. Stir up the gift which is in you and it will spring back by the Holy Spirit into life and power and fresh fuel will be added to enable you to go on to the end of the ministry that God has given you.

Spiritual character is the most vital matter in connection with Christian leadership. May God grant to us all to know this kind of character. May we be conformed to the image of His Son more and more from day to day, from year to year. And may it be true of us as it says in the book of Proverbs: "The path of the just is like a shining light that shineth yet more and more unto the noon day" (see Proverbs 4:18) May it be so with all of us.

Shall we pray?

Dear Lord, we pray that the Holy Spirit Himself will take these words, poor as they are because of the vessel, and somehow engrave them upon our hearts and in our spirits. Lord, blot out anything that is not right or that is in some way out of balance, but keep within us alive and clear all that has been spoken by Thee. Dear Lord, we pray that we might be true leaders. We know that we are living in a day when as never before leadership is required. Oh Father, raise up men and women who will be leaders amongst Thy people, who will lead then aright, who will be true pioneers and examples, who will lay down their lives for the flock, who will know the power and indwelling of the Holy Spirit. Oh Father, we pray that Thou wilt do this with all of us, and we ask it together in the name of our Lord Jesus. Amen.

Other books by Lance Lambert

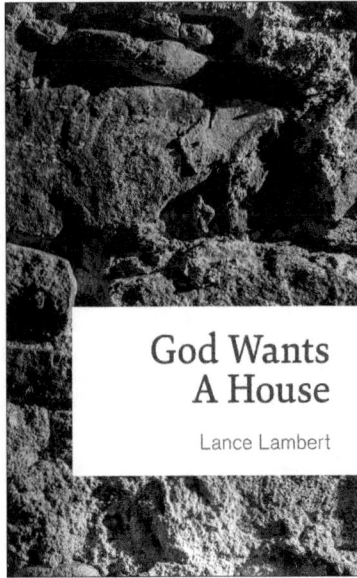

God Wants A House

Lance Lambert

God Wants A House

Where is God at home? Is He at home in Richmond, VA? Is He at home in Washington? Is He at home in Richmond, Surrey? Is He at home in these other places? Where is God at home? There are thousands of living stones, many, many dear believers with real experience of the Lord, but where has the ark come home? Where are the staves being lengthened that God has finally come home? In *God Wants a House* Lance looks into this desire of the Lord. This desire He has to dwell with His people. What would this dwelling look like? Let's seek the Lord, that we can say with David, "One thing have I asked of Jehovah, that will I seek after:that I may dwell in the house of Jehovah all the days of my life, To behold the beauty of Jehovah, And to inquire in his temple."

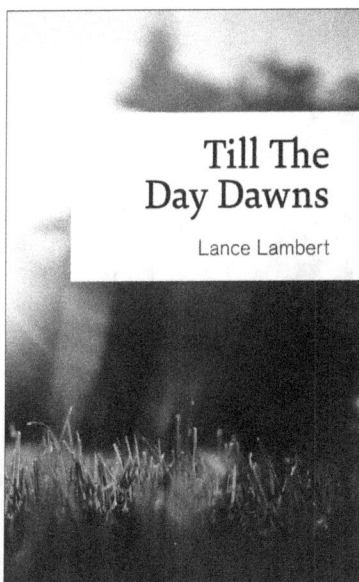

Till the Day Dawns

"And we have the word of prophecy made more sure; whereunto ye do well that ye take heed, as unto a lamp shining in a dark place, until the day dawn, and the day-star arise in your hearts." (II Peter 1:9).

The word of prophecy was not given that we might merely be comforted but that we would be prepared and made ready. Let us look into the Word of God together, searching out the prophecies, that the Day-Star arise in our hearts until the Day dawns.

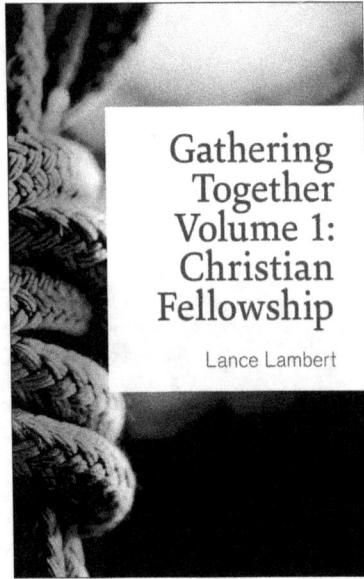

Gathering Together Volume 1

What is the church?

What is the basis for meeting together as the church?

What is true fellowship?

What is the priesthood of all believers?

What is the difference between unity
and uniformity in the church?

In this book, the first volume of *Gathering Together*, Lance Lambert answers these questions and many more. In doing this, he emphasizes the absolute headship of Christ and the oneness of the body of Christ.

www.ingramcontent.com/pod-product-compliance
Lightning Source LLC
LaVergne TN
LVHW051254080426
835509LV00020B/2977